Low Car(bon) Communities

With increasing awareness of the urgent need to respond to global warming by reducing carbon emissions and recognition of the social benefits of car-free and car-lite living, more and more city planners, advocates and everyday urban dwellers are demanding new ways of building cities. In *Low Car(bon) Communities*, authors Nicole Foletta and Jason Henderson examine seven case studies in Europe and the United States that aim explicitly to reduce dependency on cars. Innovative and inspirational, these communities provide a rich array of data and metrics for comparison and analysis. This book considers these low car(bon) communities' potential for transferability to cities around the world, including in North America.

Aimed at practicing city planners, sustainable transportation advocates and students in planning, geography and environmental studies, this book will be an invaluable benchmark for gauging the success of sustainable urban futures.

Nicole Foletta has worked in the field of transportation planning for over 10 years under a variety of contexts, from public to private sector, with experience in both Europe and the United States. Most recently she has worked as a Senior Transportation Planner at Fehr & Peers transportation consultants in San Francisco, California, USA, bringing a focus on improving communities to all of her projects. Nicole is dedicated to finding innovative solutions that promote sustainable principles.

Jason Henderson is a Geography Professor at San Francisco State University, USA. His research and teaching include transportation and land use, with an emphasis on how culture and politics shape urban transportation policy. His book *Street Fight: The Politics of Mobility in San Francisco* (2013) examines debates over freeway removal, parking, bicycle politics and transit finance.

"*Low Car(bon) Communitie*s is the antidote to car-oriented development. Through seven detailed, generously illustrated case studies of newly developed neighborhoods, Foletta and Henderson provide a viable roadmap to fight global warming with less parking and fewer cars."

—Adam Millard-Ball, University of California, Santa Cruz, USA

Low Car(bon) Communities

Inspiring car-free and car-lite urban futures

Nicole Foletta and Jason Henderson

LONDON AND NEW YORK

First published 2016
by Routledge
2 Park Square, Milton Park, Abingdon, Oxon OX14 4RN

and by Routledge
711 Third Avenue, New York, NY 10017

Routledge is an imprint of the Taylor & Francis Group, an informa business

© 2016 Nicole Foletta and Jason Henderson

The right of Nicole Foletta and Jason Henderson to be identified as authors of this work has been asserted by them in accordance with sections 77 and 78 of the Copyright, Designs and Patents Act 1988.

All rights reserved. No part of this book may be reprinted or reproduced or utilized in any form or by any electronic, mechanical, or other means, now known or hereafter invented, including photocopying and recording, or in any information storage or retrieval system, without permission in writing from the publishers.

Trademark notice: Product or corporate names may be trademarks or registered trademarks, and are used only for identification and explanation without intent to infringe.

British Library Cataloguing-in-Publication Data
A catalogue record for this book is available from the British Library

Library of Congress Cataloging-in-Publication Data
Names: Foletta, Nicole, author. | Henderson, Jason, 1972– author.
    Title: Low car(bon) communities: inspiring car-free and car-lite urban
    futures/Nicole Foletta and Jason Henderson.
    Description: 1 Edition. | New York : Routledge, 2016.
    Identifiers: LCCN 2015034696|
    Subjects: LCSH: Transportation, Automotive—Social aspects—Case studies. |
    Transportation planning—Case studies. | City planning—Case studies. |
    Community development—Environmental aspects.
    Classification: LCC HE5611 .F65 2016 | DDC 388.3/42—dc23
    LC record available at http://lccn.loc.gov/2015034696

ISBN: 978-1-138-82586-4 (pbk)
ISBN: 978-1-315-73962-5 (ebk)

Typeset in Syntax
by Florence Production Ltd, Stoodleigh, Devon, UK

Printed and bound in India by Replika Press Pvt. Ltd.

Contents

List of figures vii
List of tables ix
List of boxes x
List of photos xi
Acknowledgments xiv
List of terms xvii

1 **Introduction: why low car(bon)? Global warming, cars and cities** 1

2 **Amsterdam: GWL Terrein case study** 7

3 **Freiburg: Vauban case study** 23

4 **San Francisco: Market and Octavia case study** 40

5 **Stockholm: Hammarby Sjöstad case study** 72

6 **Malmö: Västra Hamnen case study** 91

7 **London: Greenwich Millennium Village case study** 109

8 **The Randstad: Houten case study** 125

9 **Conclusions and lessons learned** 141

Index 155

Figures

2.1	Map of GWL Terrein	10
2.2	Mode split for all trips for GWL Terrein, Amsterdam West and Amsterdam residents	20
2.3	Work mode split for GWL Terrein and Amsterdam residents	21
2.4	Comparison of transport-related emissions for residents of GWL Terrein, Amsterdam and the Netherlands	21
2.5	Importance of various factors on GWL Terrein resident decision not to own a car	22
3.1	Map of Vauban	26
3.2	Mode split for all trips for Vauban, Rieselfeld and Freiburg	34
3.3	Mode split for commute trips for Vauban and Freiburg residents	34
3.4	Mode split for shopping trips for Vauban residents	34
3.5	Mode split for leisure trips for Vauban and Freiburg residents	35
3.6	Car ownership rates for Vauban, Rieselfeld, Freiburg and Germany	35
4.1	Map of Market and Octavia	41
4.2	Car ownership rates in San Francisco, Market and Octavia, and the Marina	62
4.3	Car density in San Francisco, Market and Octavia, and the Marina	62
4.4	Commute mode shares for San Francisco, the Marina, and Market and Octavia	63
4.5	Map of San Francisco VMT per household	64
4.6	Average daily VMT for San Francisco, Market and Octavia, and the Marina	65
5.1	Map of Hammarby Sjöstad	75
5.2	Ridership on Tvärbanan line	77
5.3	The Hammarby Model	86
5.4	Transportation mode split for various regions in Stockholm County	88
5.5	Transportation mode split for Hammarby Sjöstad and reference district (2007)	88
5.6	Mode of travel to work, Hammarby Sjöstad residents (2010)	89
5.7	Comparison of car emissions for Hammarby Sjöstad and reference district	89
5.8	Comparison of transport-related emissions for residents of Hammarby Sjöstad, Stockholm and Sweden	89
6.1	Map of Västra Hamnen	94
6.2	Mode split for various trip purposes for Västra Hamnen and Malmö residents	106
6.3	Mode split for all trips for Västra Hamnen and Malmö residents	106
6.4	Distance to work for Västra Hamnen residents (2010)	107
7.1	Map of Greenwich Millennium Village	109
7.2	Cars per household in GMV and London	121
7.3	Mode split for all trips in GMV, Greenwich and London	122
7.4	Mode of travel to work for GMV residents (2005)	122
7.5	GMV resident mode of travel for various trip types (2005)	123
8.1	Map of Houten	126
8.2	Activity level of residents of the Netherlands, South Houten and Veldhuizen	136
8.3	Perceptions of bicycle path quality and safety in South Houten and Veldhuizen	136

FIGURES

8.4	Mode of travel to work for South Houten and Veldhuizen residents	137
8.5	Mode of travel to work for Houten and Milton Keynes residents	137
8.6	Mode of travel for various trip types for Houten residents (2010)	138
8.7	Mode of travel for all trips made by Houten, Zeist and Milton Keynes residents	138
9.1	Land transport-related emissions comparisons	144

Tables

1.1	Summary of existing site characteristics	4
2.1	Statistics for GWL Terrein, Amsterdam West and Amsterdam	19
3.1	Statistics for Vauban, Rieselfeld and Freiburg	33
4.1	Statistics for Market and Octavia, the Marina, and City of San Francisco	61
5.1	Summary of Hammarby Sjöstad ferry service	79
5.2	Parking prices in Hammarby Sjöstad	83
5.3	Breakdown of residential unit size in Hammarby Sjöstad	85
5.4	Statistics for Hammarby Sjöstad, Sundbyberg, Inner Stockholm and City of Stockholm	87
6.1	Parking zones for the City of Malmö	99
6.2	Emissions reductions from shift to carsharing vehicles in Malmö (2008)	99
6.3	Breakdown of residential unit size in Västra Hamnen	102
6.4	Statistics for Västra Hamnen and City of Malmö	105
6.5	Residential unit densities in various Västra Hamnen neighborhoods	105
7.1	Statistics for GMV, Greenwich and London	121
8.1	Statistics for Houten, Zeist, Milton Keynes, South Houten and Veldhuizen	135
9.1	Summary of site characteristics	141
9.2	Overview of urban design and policy features	142
9.3	Mode share and car ownership rates for study sites and reference areas	143

Boxes

2.1	GWL Terrein site facts	8
2.2	One-way carsharing	17
3.1	Vauban site facts	23
3.2	Freiburg transportation policy	24
4.1	Market and Octavia site facts	40
4.2	Planning in California	45
4.3	Parklets	54
4.4	Proposition 13	55
5.1	Hammarby Sjöstad site facts	72
5.2	Stockholm congestion charge	78
5.3	Stockholm disability program	85
6.1	Västra Hamnen site facts	92
6.2	The Øresund Bridge	98
6.3	No Ridiculous Car Journeys	103
7.1	GMV site facts	110
7.2	London congestion charge	111
7.3	Section 106 agreements	112
7.4	Oyster Card	116
8.1	City of Houten site facts	125
8.2	Filtered permeability	126
8.3	Vinex locations	127

Photos

2.1	GWL Terrein	7
2.2	Bicycle and pedestrian bridge in GWL Terrein	8
2.3	"No motorized vehicles allowed" sign in GWL Terrein	11
2.4	Bollards and raised curbs prevent motorized vehicles from entering GWL Terrein	11
2.5	Pedestrian path in GWL Terrein	11
2.6	Aerial view of GWL Terrein	12
2.7	Shared garden in GWL Terrein	13
2.8	Wheelchair-accessible residential unit in GWL Terrein	13
2.9	Cafe Amsterdam in GWL Terrein	14
2.10	Tram at Van Hallstraat Station near GWL Terrein	15
2.11	Greenwheels carsharing vehicle near GWL Terrein	16
2.12	Subterranean waste containers in GWL Terrein	19
3.1	Distinctive architecture and car-free streets in Vauban	24
3.2	Parking-free street in Vauban	25
3.3	Signage indicating shared use of street and slow traffic speeds in Vauban	27
3.4	Mixed uses: residential buildings with ground floor retail and cafes in Vauban	28
3.5	Pedestrian plaza in Vauban	28
3.6	Family bicycling in Vauban	29
3.7	Barriers to vehicle entry to pedestrian and bicycle paths in Vauban	29
3.8	Bicycle parking in front of residences in Vauban	30
3.9	Vauban tram on green track	31
3.10	Vauban tram	31
3.11	Car-free streets in Vauban	36
4.1	View of Octavia Boulevard	42
4.2	Aerial view of freeway before removal	42
4.3	View of existing freeway off-ramp onto Market Street and Octavia Boulevard	43
4.4	SF Jazz	47
4.5	SF Park curbside parking payment machine	49
4.6	Cafe and street life on Market Street	51
4.7	Residential buildings with ground floor retail and restaurants in Market and Octavia area	52
4.8	Art exhibit and children's playground on Patricia's Green in Market and Octavia area	52
4.9	Patricia's Green public plaza space in Market and Octavia area	53
4.10	Linden Street living alleyway in Market and Octavia area	53
4.11	Parklet in Market and Octavia area	55
4.12	Green bike lane and red transit-only lanes on Market Street	57
4.13	Contraflow red bus-only lane on Haight Street	58
4.14	Red bus-only lanes, green bike lane and soft-hit posts on Market Street	58
4.15	Green bike lane and bicycle counter on Market Street	59
4.16	Cycle track and bicycle signal head on Market Street	59

PHOTOS

4.17	Bike-share station and green bike lane on Market Street	59
5.1	Pedestrian pathways in Hammarby Sjöstad	73
5.2	Hammarby Sjöstad before redevelopment	74
5.3	Hammarby Sjöstad today	74
5.4	Residential mixed use in Hammarby Sjöstad	76
5.5	Tvärbanan line tram stop in Hammarby Sjöstad	77
5.6	Ferry terminal in Hammarby Sjöstad	79
5.7	Tree-lined pedestrian pathway in Hammarby Sjöstad	80
5.8	Pedestrian bridge in Hammarby Sjöstad	80
5.9	Pedestrian walkways along canal in Hammarby Sjöstad	80
5.10	Bike sharing station in Hammarby Sjöstad	81
5.11	Carsharing vehicle in Hammarby Sjöstad	81
5.12	Car2Go vehicle in Stockholm	82
5.13	Parking signage in Hammarby Sjöstad	82
5.14	Waterfront walkway in Hammarby Sjöstad	84
5.15	Cafe in Hammarby Sjöstad	84
6.1	Plaza in Västra Hamnen	91
6.2	Public walkways in Västra Hamnen	92
6.3	Turning Torso in Västra Hamnen	92
6.4	Mothers walking in pedestrian space in Västra Hamnen	96
6.5	People walking and biking near waterfront in Västra Hamnen	96
6.6	Bus in bus-only lane in Västra Hamnen	97
6.7	Cafe and plaza in Västra Hamnen	100
6.8	Västra Hamnen waterfront	101
6.9	Pedestrian ways between buildings in Västra Hamnen	101
6.10	Residential buildings in Västra Hamnen	102
6.11	Water channel in Västra Hamnen	104
7.1	Greenwich Millennium Village	110
7.2	Live/work units in GMV	112
7.3	Millennium Primary School in GMV	113
7.4	View of GMV and O2 Arena from water	114
7.5	North Greenwich station designed by Will Alsop	115
7.6	Millennium Busway in GMV	116
7.7	Green space behind residential units in GMV	117
7.8	Lake and ecology park in GMV	118
7.9	Landscaped courtyard in GMV	119
7.10	Colorful plaza in GMV	119
8.1	Bicyclist in Houten	128
8.2	Bicycle path in Houten	128

8.3	Speed bumps designed to slow motorized scooters but not bikes in Houten	129
8.4	Sign stating that bikes have priority and cars are "guests" in Houten	130
8.5	Bicycle tunnel under ring road in Houten	130
8.6	Bicycle paths and crowded bike parking in Houten	130
8.7	Bicycle paths around residential neighborhood in Houten	131
8.8	Bicycle priority at intersection in Houten	132
8.9	Bicyclists in central plaza in Houten	133
8.10	Carsharing vehicle in Houten	134
8.11	Bicycle trailer in Houten	139

Acknowledgments

The aim of this book was to provide inspiration for car-free and car-lite developments, and more broadly, making cities a stronger part of sustainable urban futures. None of this would have been possible, however, without the many colleagues who have inspired us, and who have contributed in many constructive ways to make this project happen.

NICOLE FOLETTA

First, I would like to acknowledge the Institute for Transportation and Development Policy (ITDP) for initiating this research in 2009. ITDP works around the world to design and implement high-quality transport systems and policy solutions that make cities more livable, equitable and sustainable (www.itdp.org). ITDP is a global nonprofit at the forefront of innovation, providing technical expertise to accelerate the growth of sustainable transport and urban development around the world. Through their transport projects, policy advocacy and research publications, they work to reduce carbon emissions, enhance social inclusion and improve the quality of life for people in cities.

Working with ITDP, my colleague Simon Field and I researched best practices of low car(bon) communities across Europe, including interviewing city planners and conducting travel behavior surveys of residents in several of the developments studied. I would like to give a sincere thanks to Simon Field for his work in this first phase of the project.

I would also like to express my great appreciation to my friend and co-author, Jason Henderson, for reinitiating the research with me in 2014. During this time, we updated the case studies, added a new, San Francisco-based case study and provided lessons learned for a North American audience. Jason was the ideal person to work with me on the Market and Octavia area case study in San Francisco, having lived in the area since 2003, during which time he has been highly involved in the development and monitoring of the Market and Octavia Area Plan. Jason is also a Professor of Geography at San Francisco State University, with research in mobility in cities, and has a keen perspective on how the lessons of these case studies can be deployed throughout North American cities.

A handful of multitalented professionals helped with this project and must be acknowledged. With an eye toward detail and an appreciation for visualizing data, Amy Smith created the case study maps, which are a valuable contribution to the book.

For the Amsterdam case study, GWL Terrein, I would like to thank members of the Koepelvereniging organization. First, Corine Marseille, who gave me a tour of the site and provided valuable information, as well as Diego Pos, who has provided information, data and updates on the site. Furthermore, from the City of Amsterdam, I would like to express my appreciation to Daniel van Motman and Hans Niepoth for providing information and data to help set the context for the development within the larger city. I would like to thank Giesbert Nijhuis, a resident of the development himself, and Peter Elenbaas for their photographs of GWL Terrein.

This project was greatly enhanced by the research provided by Simon Field for the Freiburg case study, Vauban. I would also like to thank Andrea Broaddus for her insight, Andreas Delleske for providing updates on the development and William Bacon for his attentive photos of Vauban.

ACKNOWLEDGMENTS

The San Francisco case study, Market and Octavia, is near and dear to my heart since I have called the San Francisco Bay Area home for over 15 years, and this is where I am a practicing transportation planner. Many of my friends and colleagues in the field have contributed time, insight, data analysis and other information for this case study. First, I thank my co-author Jason for writing the majority of the case study, for putting in many long hours and for educating me on many nuances and details of the project that I never knew. I would like to express my appreciation to Andrea Contreras of the San Francisco City Planning Department for her insight on planning policies of the city and how they impact new development, Market and Octavia in particular. I would like to thank Drew Cooper of the San Francisco County Transportation Authority for providing data analysis and graphics to help describe the VMT intensity across the city. I would like to thank Kristen Carnarius of the Metropolitan Transportation Commission for her data analysis contribution, helping to explain changes in travel patterns in the city over time.

For the Stockholm case study, Hammarby Sjöstad, I would like to thank Björn Cederquist and Daniel Firth, of the City of Stockholm, for patiently answering my endless stream of questions about the development, and Malena Karlsson of GlasHusEtt for her welcoming and thoughtful responses to questions throughout the research process. I would like to thank my good friends Carleton Wong and Adrienne Miller for so beautifully documenting the development through photographs.

For the Malmö case study, Västra Hamnen, I would like to thank Csaba Gyarmati and Magnus Fahl from the City of Malmö for their tireless efforts to help me distribute a survey to residents and for providing information about the development and Camilla Morland for her thorough and responsive answers to my questions.

I would like to express my great appreciation to Herbert Tiemens for giving me a bike tour of the town of Houten in order to experience this "Biker's Paradise" for myself, first hand. I would like to thank both Herbert and Frank-Jos Braspenning for providing information about the town and its planning process, and for helping to distribute a travel behavior survey to residents. I would also like to give many thanks to Professor Peter Furth, of Northeastern University, who teaches a course on the Sustainable Transportation of Holland, which features Houten, for his insightful review of my case study, which helped to provide a more in-depth analysis of the town's unique features.

Each case study site has its own story, and I'm truly grateful for the connections I have made at each and the persons in each city who have contributed their time and knowledge to help me better understand and communicate the story behind each development project.

Finally, I would like to thank my friends, family, partner and employer for supporting me through the process of compiling these stories, maps, photos and data visualizations, in a way that captures their intentions, essence and accomplishments, and lays out a path forward for other cities to learn from. We hope this book will help to educate, motivate and inspire current and future urban planners.

Nicole Foletta, December 2015

ACKNOWLEDGMENTS

JASON HENDERSON

Echoing Nicole's sentiments regarding the generous assistance in compiling this volume, we especially thank the editorial staff at Routledge for their patience. My part in this would not have been possible without generous intellectual space provided at SF State University by Sheldon Axler, Dean of the College of Science and Engineering, and Jerry Davis, Chair of the Department of Geography and Environment. I also thank my friend and fellow traveler Nicole, who invited me to participate in this inspirational project and patiently sifted through some of my more jaded narratives to produce a thoughtful and refreshingly optimistic book. Lastly, in cities around the world, tireless "street fighters"—citizen activists, planners and politicians that get it—have expanded our notion of possibilities and provide inspiration and hope. Thank you and keep up the fight!

Jason Henderson, December 2015

Terms

BIKE SHARING

The bike sharing concept consists of providing public bicycles, available from docking stations spread throughout a city, for the purpose of travel. The idea behind this initiative is to shift short-distance travel from car to bike, a sustainable and non-motorized means of transportation. Bike sharing programs are being implemented around the world to make biking in cities more accessible. These systems are often complemented by investments in bicycle infrastructure, providing safe spaces for users to ride. Positive effects of bike sharing policies on the environment, congestion problems and health have long been recognized, and there is a current trend in U.S. cities to implement such systems. In 2008, Paris won the ITDP Sustainable Award for its revolutionary bike sharing program, Vélib', the first one of its kind in a major city.

BROWNFIELD AND GREYFIELD

Brownfield is a term used in urban planning to describe land previously used for industrial purposes or some commercial uses. Such land may have been contaminated with hazardous waste or pollution, or is feared to be so. Once cleaned up, such an area can become host to new redevelopment projects. Similar to brownfields, greyfields are parking lots and low-rise, low-density strip shopping centers that can be redeveloped for denser infill development. In the United States, brownfields and greyfields hold tremendous potential for creating car-free and car-lite communities.

BUS RAPID TRANSIT

Bus rapid transit (BRT) is a high-quality bus-based transit system that delivers fast, comfortable and cost-effective services at capacities normally associated with heavy rail metros or rapid transit. It does this through the provision of dedicated lanes, with busways and iconic stations typically aligned to the center of the road, off-board fare collection, and fast and frequent operations (www.itdp.org/library/standards-and-guides/the-bus-rapid-transit-standard/what-is-brt/).

CAR-FREE

Car-free developments are blocks, neighborhoods or districts in which automobile traffic is heavily restricted. Restrictions may be full- or part-time and often include exceptions for delivery vehicles or persons with disabilities. The developments typically provide high-quality pedestrian and bicycle facilities to encourage walking and biking. Furthermore, to discourage residents from owning cars, housing developments often provide measures such as priced or rationed parking.

CAR-LITE

Car-lite development is similar to, but not as restrictive as, car-free development. Blocks, neighborhoods or districts are designed for minimal automobile use, but not full exclusion. Traffic-calming measures may be implemented in these areas to reduce traffic speeds and volumes.

CARSHARING

Carsharing is a form of car rental designed to serve as a substitute for car ownership by making cars conveniently available and charging for use by the hour or minute, with fuel and insurance included in the rates. Carsharing services locate vehicles in networks of vehicles, so that when the closest vehicle to a user is in use, another may be close by. Trips must be scheduled and vehicles are typically returned to the same location where they were picked up.

Because car usage is paid for on a per trip basis rather than through purchase, research in both Europe and North America has shown that members use cars when they are the most appropriate for the intended trip, and use other travel modes, such as public transit, walking and bicycling, more frequently. Research has also shown that a substantial number of carsharing members either sell or avoid buying a car altogether, and that total distance traveled in private, single-occupancy vehicles is reduced—benefiting society and reducing overall transportation costs for the user (Dave Brook, Carsharing Consultant, Team Red US, www.team-red.us).

Peer-to-peer carsharing is a variant of traditional carsharing in which the company manages the rental of privately owned vehicles when they are not being used by the owner. Another new carsharing model that is becoming more widely available is one-way carsharing models (see Box 2.2), increasing mobility options, which complements public transit, bicycling and walking.

FILTERED PERMEABILITY

See Box 8.2.

GREENHOUSE GASES

Greenhouse gases are gases that contribute to the greenhouse effect by absorbing infrared radiation, including carbon dioxide and chlorofluorocarbons. These gases trap heat and make the planet warmer, contributing to climate change. One of the largest sources of greenhouse gas emissions is transportation, primarily from burning fossil fuels in our cars, trucks, shops, trains and planes (www.epa.gov/climatechange/ghgemissions/).

HOUSEHOLD VEHICLE OWNERSHIP RATE

Household vehicle ownership rate, like per capita vehicle ownership, can provide useful benchmarks for comparing the case studies with one another and with their respective cities and countries. Household vehicle ownership includes the number of passenger cars, vans and light trucks available for the use of household members (see www2.census.gov/programs-surveys/acs/tech_docs/subject_definitions/2013_ACSSubjectDefinitions.pdf).

INFILL

Infill development is the process of developing vacant or underused parcels within existing urban areas that are already largely developed. Most communities have significant land within city limits, which, for various reasons, has been passed over in the normal course of urbanization. Developing this land provides opportunities to place new housing, jobs and services near the urban core, where their resource use will be less intensive.

ITDP
The Institute for Transportation and Development Policy (ITDP) is a global nonprofit at the forefront of innovation, providing technical expertise to accelerate the growth of sustainable transport and urban development around the world. Through their transport projects, policy advocacy and research publications, ITDP works to reduce carbon emissions, enhance social inclusion and improve quality of life for people in cities.

MIXED USE
Mixed-use development is, in a broad sense, any urban, suburban or village development, or even development within a single building, that blends a combination of residential, commercial, cultural, institutional or industrial uses, where those functions are physically and functionally integrated, and that provides pedestrian connections. Benefits of mixed use include: greater housing variety and density; reduced distances between housing, workplaces, retail businesses and other destinations; more compact development; stronger neighborhood character; and pedestrian- and bicycle-friendly environments. Mixing uses enables residents to walk or bike to goods and services to meet their daily needs, thus reducing distances traveled and the need to use a car.

MODE SHARE
A mode share (also referred to as mode split or modal split) is the percentage of travelers using a particular type of transportation or the number of trips using that type of transportation. Mode share is a typical metric used to measure the level of transportation sustainability in a neighborhood, city or region. Many cities have set mode share targets for balanced and sustainable transportation use. The modes of travel typically included in a mode share analysis include walking, bicycling, public transportation and private motor vehicle (sometimes specifying whether the trip was a drive-alone trip or a trip made with multiple passengers in the vehicle). Mode share targets usually reflect a desire to shift trips toward increased use of sustainable modes such as walking, bicycling and public transportation. Mode share data are typically obtained through travel surveys, which may collect information on all trips taken, or specifically on trips to work, commonly referred to as commute trips.

PER CAPITA VEHICLE OWNERSHIP RATE
Per capita vehicle ownership rates are typically calculated as the number of private vehicles (cars, light trucks, vans) owned per 1,000 persons. Ownership rates are useful for comparing nations' and cities' level of motorization. Transportation historian David Jones (2008) suggests that "mass motorization" occurs when a nation reaches a per capita of 400 motorized vehicles per 1,000 persons.

All of the case studies are located in countries with mass motorization, and the actual case studies all exhibit rates of motorization far lower than their respective countries.

In addition to usefulness for comparison, per capita vehicle ownership provides an indication of levels of motorized travel and can inform transportation decision-making and planning.

SMART GROWTH
Smart growth is an urban planning and transportation theory that concentrates growth in compact walkable urban centers to avoid sprawl. This approach supports local economies and protects the environment (www.smartgrowthamerica.org/what-is-smart-growth).

TRAFFIC CALMING
Definitions of traffic calming vary, but they all share the goal of reducing vehicle speeds, improving safety and enhancing quality of life. This may include implementation of physical measures such as edge lines, chicanes, bulb-outs, traffic circles, speed bumps and raised crosswalks to reduce traffic speeds, as well as changes to street alignment or installation of barriers to reduce cut-through traffic. (http://trafficcalming.org/).

TRANSIT-ORIENTED DEVELOPMENT
Transit-oriented development (TOD) is the creation of compact, walkable, mixed-use communities centered around high-quality train systems. This makes it possible to live a lower-stress life without complete dependence on a car for mobility needs (www.transitorienteddevelopment.org/).

UNBUNDLED PARKING
The cost of parking for residential and commercial units is often passed on to the occupants indirectly through the rent or purchase price ("bundled") rather than directly through a separate charge. For example, a three-bedroom unit might come with two parking spaces included in the purchase price or rent. This means that tenants or owners are not able to purchase only as much parking as they need, and are not given the opportunity to save money by using fewer parking spaces. The alternative is to unbundle parking—rent or sell parking spaces separately, rather than automatically including them with building space. This is not only more equitable, but can also reduce the total amount of parking required for the building.

VMT
A performance measure used to quantify the amount of travel is vehicle miles traveled (VMT). VMT is defined by the U.S. government as a measure of miles traveled by vehicles in a specified region or a specified time period. VMT is also an important input to GHG analysis since the amount of travel and conditions under which the travel occurs directly relate to how much fuel vehicles burn. One combusted gallon of gas from a vehicle is equal to approximately 24 pounds of carbon dioxide. Given today's average vehicle fuel mileage (i.e., approximately 22 miles per gallon), one mile of travel equates to about one pound of carbon dioxide. As a result, increases in VMT directly cause increases in greenhouse gas emissions and air pollution.

VMT measurement has one primary limitation: it is not directly observed and therefore cannot be directly measured. It is calculated based on the number of cars multiplied by the distance traveled by each car. The amount of VMT can be obtained through extensive surveys of residents, visitors and employees, or using a validated travel demand model that estimates vehicle demand. VMT estimates derived from travel demand forecasting models are dependent on the level of detail in the network and other variables related to vehicle movement through the network. The volume of traffic and distance traveled depends on land use types, density/intensity and patterns, as well as the supporting transportation system.

REFERENCE

Jones, D. W. (2008) *Mass Motorization and Mass Transit: An American History and Policy Analysis*, Bloomington, IN: Indiana University Press.

1
Introduction

Why low car(bon)? Global warming, cars and cities

Low car(bon) refers to communities that offer paths to significant reductions in carbon and other greenhouse gas (GHG) emissions by limiting and discouraging car use and car ownership. These intentional communities can be "car-free," with heavy restrictions on car use or car ownership, such as streets closed to car traffic and measures such as priced or rationed parking. "Car-lite" development is similar, but not as restrictive as car-free development. Traffic calming measures may be implemented in these areas to reduce traffic speeds and volumes, but cars are allowed.

The time for building low car(bon), car-free and car-lite communities has never been more urgent. Global GHG emissions need to peak in 2020 (some say 2016) and then decline if a safe target of 2°C warming above preindustrial times is to be met (IEA 2013).[1] This target could be achieved by reducing current global carbon emissions by 2–3 percent per year, thus avoiding a future "trillionth ton" of cumulative carbon emissions (Foster 2013). But this requires keeping a substantial portion of known fossil fuels in the ground and a significant shift toward energy conservation.

Current voluntary emissions reduction pledges are helpful, but not even close to sufficient. The World Bank (2012) frets that the lack of a universal cooperative global climate policy will result in temperature rises exceeding a disastrous 4°C increase within this century—perhaps as early as 2060. Meanwhile, transportation is not only 22 percent of the global total, but is also the fastest growing sector of global GHG emissions, forecast to grow by 40 percent by 2035 (IEA 2013). Such growth largely results from the expansion of global automobility; presently, 500 million passenger cars are in use, but by 2030 this figure is expected to reach one billion, accompanied by another billion trucks, motorcycles and other motorized vehicles (including electric bikes).

Global automobility and transport GHG emissions have also been highly uneven, considering that the United States, which has 4 percent of the world's population but 21 percent of the world's cars, produces 45 percent of the global carbon emissions that come from cars, and overall produces 25 percent of the total global GHG emissions while consuming 23 percent of the world's oil annually (USDOE 2011). If China had the same per capita car ownership rate as the United States, there would be more than one billion cars in China today—double the current worldwide rate.[2] Meanwhile, within U.S. metropolitan areas, car ownership is one of the biggest factors contributing to household GHG emissions, and the low density bands of suburbs that encircle denser urban cores have the highest proportion of emissions (Jones and Kammen 2014). In sprawling suburbs with high rates of car ownership, transportation-related emissions are more than double the household emissions in urban cores (Jones and Kammen 2014).

As the United States and other developed nations expect China, India and other developing nations to realistically participate in climate change mitigation, America will need not only to provide leadership, but also to decrease its appetite for excessive, on-demand, high-speed and long-distance automobility—and the spaces that induce driving. An incremental adaptation of allegedly clean automobility is not enough. With mass automobility having a host of negative effects, one energy scholar asks that if doctors should not encourage low-tar cigarettes, why do environmentalists encourage hybrid (or electric) cars (Zehner 2012)?

If the world's fleet of gasoline-powered automobiles shifts to electric, hydrogen fuel cells, or biofuels, the change will also draw resources away from industrial, residential and food systems, or it will have to involve an entirely new layer of energy production. Massive quantities of petroleum will be needed to scale up to wind turbines, solar panels and other cleaner energy sources. Untenable amounts of GHGs will continue to be emitted just to replace the existing petroleum-based automobile system, and the world will still hit atmospheric carbon levels of 600 to 1,000 parts per million (and maybe even higher) within this century (exceeding 420 ppm is considered unsafe for the planet, although some argue 350 ppm is unacceptable) (Intergovernmental Panel on Climate Change 2013). Moreover, future emissions from automobiles do not include the full life cycle of automobiles, which themselves contribute to substantial emissions and fossil fuel consumption (Chester and Horvath 2009). Mitigation must include scaling away from large-scale energy system approaches as a transport solution, and proactively organizing cities in a way that substantially reduces driving.

Reflecting this necessity, people and organizations throughout the world are rethinking the connection between mobility and cities. In the United States, the livability movement seeks to reduce car use by reconfiguring urban space into walkable built forms, with dense and transit-oriented development patterns associated with smart growth or new urbanism. The movement argues that Americans must undertake a considerable restructuring and rescaling of how they organize transportation in cities, and calls for reductions in annual VMT (vehicle miles traveled)—that is, less driving in order to address global-scale GHG emissions, reduce oil consumption and address a plethora of other social and environmental problems stemming from high VMT (Ewing et al. 2008). Some suggest a need to redesign American cities to reduce driving by 25–50 percent of present levels by 2050, an enterprise that will require urban freeway repurposing, reduced and priced parking, and replacement of road space with other uses (Newman et al. 2009).

At the urban scale, reducing VMT is a vexing and contentious affair because it means reallocating street space by prioritizing space for people using transit, walking and riding bicycles while limiting the space allocated to private automobiles and potentially increasing congestion and delays for people driving. It also means reshaping land use regulations and incentives to produce new housing and commercial development with the right amount of parking made available to residents and visitors. Parking caps (known as maximums) and allowing zero parking (zero minimums) are some of the most ambitious examples of policy and development changes to create low car(bon) communities.

There are examples of places where these shifts are occurring, and in this book we look to these places because they may be at the cutting edge in reducing transportation GHG emissions by reallocating street space and promoting compact, car-free or car-lite development. Among our examples are cities with large swaths of "brownfields," former industrial areas that have been rezoned for intensive residential and commercial infill development centered on transit and walkability.

CASE STUDIES

We use a case study approach, which is a research methodology that contributes to an understanding of complex social phenomena involved in debates over cities and urban space (Yin 1994). Multiple sources of evidence—archival documentation, interviews, direct observation—are strengths of case study research used in this book. Using multiple sources of evidence, these case studies are examined to identify converging lines of inquiry where multiple sources of evidence points to what works and what doesn't. A case study approach is not new to urban planning literature. Key works using a case study approach include *Green Urbanism* (Beatley 2000), *The Transit Metropolis* (Cervero 1998) The End of Automobile Dependence (Newman and Kenworthy 2015) and *Sustainability and Cities: Overcoming Automobile Dependence* (Newman and Kenworthy 1999).

In the following chapters, we provide case studies of seven exemplary low car(bon) communities. For each study, we discuss the impetus around how each development came to be. We then describe the key policy and design measures incorporated into each site that help to facilitate low car(bon) lifestyles. A quantitative analysis is also included, summarizing available statistics related to car use and ownership (many coming from resident travel surveys conducted by one of the authors of this book through ITDP in 2010) of both the study site and a reference district in order to provide perspective regarding the difference in travel choices of residents in communities where sustainable policies and design measures have been implemented versus otherwise similar areas that have not implemented such measures. Finally, lessons learned for each case study are presented.

The case studies are primarily pulled from Western Europe, with one in the United States. The first three case studies exhibit high levels of participatory process and attempt to integrate innovative car-free or car-lite developments into the existing urban fabric. We start with GWL Terrein, located in Amsterdam, itself recognized around the world as a bike-first city. Among the case study sites, we feel that GWL Terrein has gone the furthest to reduce the role of the car in people's lives, while ensuring that an urban, car-free lifestyle is affordable to a diverse array of residents.

The next case study, Vauban, located in Freiburg, Germany, is a car-free development on an urban infill site that was influenced by strong local advocacy and a commitment by citizens to create a sustainable urban development. The third case study site is our U.S. example, located in San Francisco, California. Since our target audience in this book is on North American applications, we go into more depth with this case study, describing many of the political factors involved in development planning and implementation. The Market and Octavia Plan sets an ambitious focus on reducing car dependency, facilitated through progressive parking regulations, among other measures. The lessons learned are particularly relevant for other U.S. and Canadian cities hoping to address the issues of increasing automobility in cities.

The next three case studies are examples of showcase developments primarily developed as part of a national agenda to promote environmental sustainability. All three are urban port or waterfront redevelopments near the city center. The first of these three, Hammarby Sjöstad, located in Stockholm, Sweden, is an internationally recognized example of a district planning approach incorporating sustainable resource use, ecological design and low carbon transportation. Västra Hamnen, also located in Sweden in the city of Malmö, is similarly recognized for incorporating progressive policies and measures to reduce car dependency with investments in modern, signature architecture. Greenwich Millennium Village, in London, although not as ideally located as the other case study sites, has implemented a progressive parking strategy and places strict requirements on developers to invest in measures that contribute to the sustainability of the development and offset negative externalities.

Table 1.1 Summary of existing site characteristics

City	Development	Current population	Developed area (acres)	Residential units	Population density (persons/ acre)	Parking spaces per residential unit	Distance from city center (miles)
Amsterdam	GWL Terrein	1,400	15	600	95	0.22	1.8
Freiburg	Vauban	5,500	100	2,470	55	< 0.5	2
San Francisco	Market and Octavia	30,800	740	19,100	42	< 0.6	1.5
Stockholm	Hammarby Sjöstad	20,000	400	10,000	50	0.65	2
Malmö	Västra Hammen	7,000	215	4,000	33	0.8	1.2
London	Greenwich Millennium Village	2,300	50	1,095	46	0.7	5
Houten	Houten	48,000	2,030	18,400	24	1.1	5*

* Distance from Utrecht city center

The final case study site, Houten in the Netherlands, is a unique example of an entire masterplanned city designed to facilitate inner-city travel by bicycle. It is also different from the other case studies in that it is a suburban greenfield development. While the most effective locations for redevelopment to address the issues of growing VMT and GHG emissions discussed above are in urban infill locations, lessons can be gained from Houten regarding design measures and policies that can be implemented in suburban locations in the United States.

Basic characteristics of the seven case study sites are summarized in Table 1.1.

TRANSFERABILITY

The low carbon communities examined here should be seen as inspirational and examined for their potential for transferability, especially to North American cities, but also globally. There are indications that long-term, many of the ideas can be incorporated incrementally but also broadly. For example, throughout North America, there is a bicycle renaissance (Pucher and Buehler 2011) whereby more and more cities are steering resources toward bicycle infrastructure and policies that support bicycle use. Parking policy is also undergoing reform as the work of Donald Shoup (2005) has convinced more cities to reform parking standards and how curbside space is managed. Cities lead by example, and the more cities that take on a low car(bon) approach, the more likely others will follow. To be sure, political culture must be amicable to change, and so we acknowledge that change will not happen overnight. But many cities have the following characteristics worth considering.

An increasing number of U.S. cities, beyond Portland or New York, have emerging transit-first or walk-first policies whereby investment in transit, bicycling and walking are prioritized over roads and cars. In California, San Francisco and Los Angeles have explicit policies calling for transit-oriented development, and statewide, the state's regional planning laws require explicit reductions in VMT as part of metropolitan planning.

U.S. cities all exhibit some stage of deindustrialization, as manufacturing is shifted offshore or to the suburbs, and as port technology is shifted from bulk cargo to containerization. From Boston and San Diego, large swaths of land adjacent to city centers are prime for low car(bon) style development. In North America, these key, often centrally located sites are called "brownfields." As well, many cities are considering freeway removal in the urban core, which, as seen in our San Francisco case study, opens up land for redevelopment into walkable neighborhoods with good access to city centers and transit.

In the United States, a renewed appreciation for cities and culture of urbanism is seen among "millennials" and empty nesters. There is a strong desire for urban living, and younger people are either deferring or avoiding car ownership altogether. Politically, many U.S. cities have a local electorate supportive of tax increases for transit and bicycle infrastructure, and this is especially relevant since local taxes increasingly fund capital improvements, while the federal government has retreated on financing for massive new highways, and instead emphasis is on maintenance and system stabilization. There are some who suggest that VMT and sprawl have peaked in the United States and that we may be on the verge of a dramatic recentralization and densification of both central cities and older suburbs (Millard-Ball and Schipper 2010; Barrington-Leigh and Millard-Ball 2015). Old shopping malls surrounded by acres of surface parking can be easily reconfigured into vibrant mixed-use communities—sometimes referred to as "greyfields."

Increased fuel prices and fuel price volatility will also be a factor. When prices spiked in 2008, many households in car-dependent suburbs were hit hardest, and property values plummeted in the places where there was no choice but to drive. Lastly, with increased awareness and acceptance of the urgency of global warming, we do believe that most U.S. adults are mature enough to understand that how we get around does matter, and that individual choice and responsibility, while not the panacea, does have an impact. With that in mind, we hope to inspire and motivate people to reconsider how cities are built in North America, one neighborhood at a time. If we are successful, future generations will thank our generation of planners and urbanists for appreciating the urgency of our time.

NOTES

1. Recent science suggests that 2°C above the 1900 global mean is a tolerable temperature window, or threshold, for averting social and economic disruption to human systems due to climate change (Hansen et al. 2008).
2. In 2009, the United States had 828 vehicles per 1,000 people. Given its population in 2012 of 1.343 billion and that rate of car ownership, China would have over 1.112 billion vehicles. Data on vehicles are from USDOE (2011: Table 3.5); China population figure is from www.census.gov/population/international/data/idb/country.php.

REFERENCES

Barrington-Leigh, C. and Millard-Ball, A. (2015) "A century of sprawl in the United States," *PNAS*, 112(27): 8244–8249, published ahead of print, June 15.

Beatley, T. (2000) *Green Urbanism: Learning from European Cities*, Washington, DC: Island Press.

Cervero, R. (1998) *The Transit Metropolis: A Global Inquiry*, Washington, DC: Island Press.

Chester, M. and Horvath, A. (2009) "Environmental assessment of passenger transportation should include infrastructure and supply chains," *Environmental Research Letters*, 4: 1–8.

Ewing, R., Bartholomew, K., Winkleman, S., Walters, J. and Chen, D. (2008) *Growing Cooler: The Evidence on Urban Development and Climate Change*, Washington, DC: Urban Land Institute.

Foster, J. B. (2013) "James Hansen and the climate-change exit strategy," *Monthly Review*, 64(9): 1–19.

Hansen, J. M. S., Kharecha, P., Beerling, D., Berner, R., Masson-Delmotte, V., Pagani, M. and Zachos, J. C. (2008) "Target atmospheric CO2: where should humanity aim?" *The Open Atmospheric Science Journal*, 2: 217–231.

Intergovernmental Panel on Climate Change (IPCC) (2013) *Climate Change 2013: The Physical Science Basis, Summary for Policymakers*, Geneva, CH: United Nations Environment Program and the World Meteorological Society.

International Energy Agency (IEA) (2013) *CO2 Emissions from Fuel Combustion Highlights 2013*, Paris: International Energy Agency.

Jones, C. and Kammen, D. M. (2014) "Spatial Distribution of U.S. Household Carbon Footprints Reveals Suburbanization Undermines Greenhouse Gas Benefits of Urban Population Density," *Environmental Science & Technology*, 48(2): 895–902.

Millard-Ball, A. and Schipper, L. (2010) "Are we reaching peak travel? Trends in passenger transport in eight industrialized countries," *Transport Reviews*, 31(3): 357–78.

Newman, P. and Kenworthy, J. (1999) *Sustainability and Cities: Overcoming Automobile Dependence*, Washington, DC: Island Press.

Newman, P. and Kenworthy, J. (2015) *The End of Automobile Dependence: How Cities are Moving Beyond Car-Based Planning*, Washington, DC: Island Press.

Newman, P., Beatley, T. and Boyer, H. (2009) *Resilient Cities: Responding to Peak Oil and Climate Change*, Washington, DC: Island Press.

Pucher, J. and Buehler, R. (2012) *City Cycling*, Cambridge, MA: MIT Press.

Shoup, D. (2005) *The High Cost of Free Parking*, Chicago, IL: Planners Press, American Planning Association.

United States Department of Energy (USDOE) (2011) *Transportation Energy Data Book: Edition 30*, Oak Ridge, TN: Center for Transportation Analysis, Engineering Science and Technology Division, Oak Ridge National Laboratory.

World Bank (2012) *Turn Down the Heat: Why a 4 Degree Celsius Warmer World Must Be Avoided*, Washington, DC: World Bank.

Yin, R. K. (1994). *Case Study Research: Design and Methods*, Thousand Oaks, CA: Sage.

Zehner, O. (2012) *Green Illusions: The Dirty Secret of Clean Energy and the Future of Environmentalism*, Lincoln, NE: University of Nebraska Press.

2
Amsterdam
GWL Terrein case study

BACKGROUND

GWL Terrein is located in the famously bicycling-friendly city of Amsterdam. Among the developments we have studied, GWL Terrein has gone the furthest to reduce the role of the car in people's lives. It is a car-free development at a human scale that is well connected to the fabric of the surrounding neighborhoods. While located in a desirable, trendy part of the city, GWL Terrein has managed to avoid issues of gentrification threatening the social equity of many of the other projects discussed. The development has a mix of income levels and includes social housing, ensuring that people of all income levels can enjoy urban livability and a car-free lifestyle. Many livable cities are becoming increasingly expensive, putting a premium on housing prices and making it challenging for lower-income households to be able to live in them. One of the reasons for the success of GWL Terrein, particularly in this aspect, may be its humble and modest design; it is an innovative and ambitious experiment in sustainable living, yet does so in a way that is unostentatious and respectful of the people who live there.

GWL Terrein is a car-free brownfield redevelopment with limited parking, carsharing provision and good transit access. Non-motorized mode share in the development is much higher than the surrounding

Photo 2.1

GWL Terrein

2: AMSTERDAM: GWL TERREIN CASE STUDY

Photo 2.2
Bicycle and pedestrian bridge in GWL Terrein

**BOX 2.1
GWL TERREIN SITE FACTS**

Developer:
Ecoplan Foundation

Architect:
Kees Christiaanse

Population:
1,400

Area:
15 acres

Density:
95 persons/acre

Residential units:
600

Construction began:
1995

Construction completed:
1998

Distance from city center:
1.8 miles

Cars:
190 cars/1,000 residents

Parking spaces/residence:
0.20

Non-motorized mode share:
80%

Public transit mode share:
14%

Households with carsharing:
26%

area and car use is much lower. The project is situated in the Amsterdam West District, less than two miles from the city center at the terminus of a tram line and the very edge of the late nineteenth-century city extensions. It makes use of a 15-acre site formerly used by the municipal water utility, Gemeente Waterleidingen (GWL), from which it gets its name. Local residents were involved in the design and development of the project. They wanted to push forward with a new approach to development with a focus on car-free living, reuse of resources, conservation of energy and water, and community cohesion.

The inner area of the development is car-free and only emergency vehicles are allowed on-site. The initial residents were asked to sign a non-obligatory declaration of support for the car-free nature of the site. None of the 600 residential units include parking spaces; however, several public on-street parking spaces are located along the edge of the development and a limited number of parking permits are available for residents. In this way, residents are able to own cars, but many choose not to.

GWL Terrein's environmental and social goals make it a unique place to live. The car-free inner area creates a cleaner, safer place for neighbors to interact and children to play. The focus on energy-efficient building design and promotion of sustainable transportation helps reduce the carbon footprint of residents. Furthermore, the work of the residential umbrella organization encourages focus on sustainable living and community involvement. It is no surprise that the development consistently receives high satisfaction ratings from residents, which is further underscored by the fact that 62 percent of residents have lived in the development for more than eight years (www.gwl-terrein.nl/?english). Once residents move here, they don't seem to want to leave. What began as an idealistic experiment in combining high-density housing with green principles appears to have produced a neighborhood its original proponents can be proud of, even 15 years later.

PLANNING PROCESS

GWL Terrein used to be the site of the Municipal Water Company. When the water company decided to move, residents of what was then the Westerpark District (now part of the Amsterdam West District) lobbied for the location to become a residential area, while companies operating nearby wanted the location to be zoned for industrial purposes. The residents won out, and in 1989 the Amsterdam City Council decided to zone the area for housing. Local residents remained actively involved in the decision process and appealed for a car-free eco-district. This idea was also supported by politicians and the local community center.

In 1993, the basic principles for the site were described in an Urban Planning Schedule of Requirements. The site was to be car-free and aimed to discourage car ownership and use by ensuring good public transit, a safe environment for pedestrians and selecting inhabitants who agreed with the ecological principles of the project. Environmental goals also included reduction in water and energy consumption. In addition, it was decided that half of the dwellings would be reserved as renter-occupied, social housing. The other half would be sold, two-thirds of which would be grant-aided owner-occupied dwellings. Furthermore, local residents would have priority in applying for dwellings.

The Westerpark Urban District commissioned two architecture firms to make an idea sketch for the development based on the Urban Planning Schedule of Requirements. In August 1993, the plan made by architect Kees Christiaanse and landscape designer Adriaan Geuze was chosen by a panel consisting of several inhabitants, representatives of the Westerpark Urban District and the project developer. This panel, along with the architect, then collaborated to create an Urban Plan for the development, which was completed in November 1993. The Environmental Advisory Bureau BOOM was also involved in the process to ensure that the environmental aspects of the Urban Planning Schedule of Requirements were upheld.

Private investors were not interested in developing the site, given the strict environmental requirements proposed. In the end, five housing associations set up the Ecoplan Foundation as a joint venture to coordinate and finance the development. Future inhabitants continued to be involved in the design process. In 1994, five design teams were formed to design various sections of the development, each with an architect and several inhabitants. Construction took place in three phases, starting in 1995 and ending in 1998 (www.gwl-terrein.nl/?english).

KEY POLICY AND DESIGN MEASURES

From the start, GWL Terrein had a focus on reduced car usage and sustainable living. These sentiments came from local residents of the Westerpark District itself and were supported by the local government. Beyond its car-free nature, several other policy and design strategies have been incorporated into the site to promote these ideals. These are described below.

Urban design

As mentioned, the entire 15-acre site of GWL Terrein is car-free. The development consists of 17 mid- and high-rise apartment buildings along with the renovated pump engine building, which is now home to Cafe Amsterdam. The buildings are arranged to form a high-density perimeter, while the inner areas remain open, including plenty of green public spaces, wide pathways and safe areas for children to play.

2: AMSTERDAM: GWL TERREIN CASE STUDY

Figure 2.1

Map of GWL Terrein

Source: Map by Amy Smith

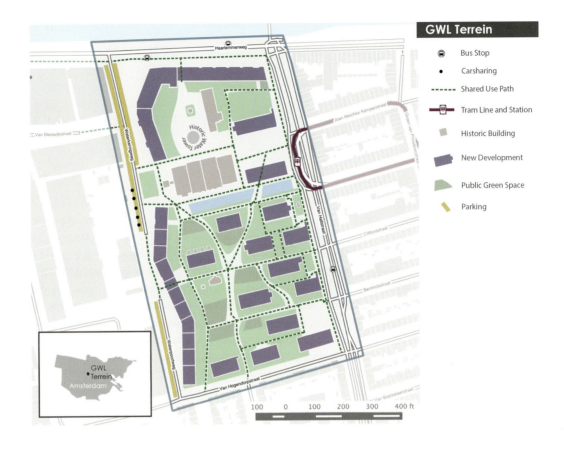

STREET LAYOUT AND DESIGN

Since cars are not allowed on-site, no streets pass through the development. Furthermore, signs are posted at various entrance points, stating that no motorized vehicles are allowed on the site. In order to enforce this, the development is raised from street level so that cars do not have access to the inner area. However, ramped access points are located at certain entrances to the development, and sometimes motorized two-wheelers illegally enter the development. Police officers patrol the area to limit these infractions.

Van Hallstraat, an arterial street at the eastern border of GWL Terrein, was traffic-calmed in 1999 with on-street parking removed, speed reduced, sidewalks widened and the tram terminus rebuilt and extended (Scheurer 2001). Bordering GWL Terrein on this street is a brick-colored bicycle lane. Near the tram terminus, this bicycle lane is bordered by the tram platform and two tram lanes. Beyond the tram lanes are two lanes of traffic, followed by car parking and another bicycle lane at the furthest side of the street. For the rest of Van Hallstraat, the bicycle lane bordering GWL Terrein is protected by a tree-lined median. Beyond this median are two car lanes. At the far side of the street is a lane for car parking and another bicycle path. In this way, bicycle lanes are protected from moving traffic either by a row of trees, a tram platform or a strip of parked cars.

PUBLIC SPACE DESIGN

A variety of public spaces are available between the buildings, including public green spaces, children's play areas, shared gardens and mixed-use pathways. This is important, since in such a high-density development, it is impossible to provide each residential unit with a private yard. Beyond being a more efficient use of space, these shared spaces provide residents with more chances to interact, building their sense of community.

2: AMSTERDAM: GWL TERREIN CASE STUDY

Photo 2.3 *(top left)*

"No motorized vehicles allowed" sign in GWL Terrein

Photo 2.4 *(top right)*

Bollards and raised curbs prevent motorized vehicles from entering GWL Terrein

Photo 2.5 *(left)*

Pedestrian path in GWL Terrein

2: AMSTERDAM: GWL TERREIN CASE STUDY

Photo 2.6

Aerial view of GWL Terrein

Source: Photo by Peter Elenbaas (www.onbewolkt.nl)

An artificial canal effectively divides the development into two parts. To the north is an urban square surrounded by a nine-story residential building with ground floor retail. To the south, the site is more garden-oriented, with open green spaces and children's play areas. The children's play areas are located away from the street and have been praised by many families as being safe places where their children can play near home. In addition, several shared garden allotments are provided, which are surrounded by a protective wall of shrubbery. Within these spaces, residents can rent a garden allotment. The gardens give residents another opportunity to interact with neighbors and also provide residents with a sense of ownership for the public spaces.

The internal area does not have any dedicated bicycle lanes, but rather provides wide, mixed-use pathways, shared by pedestrians and bicyclists. One perspective is that this mix of uses can actually improve safety because both bicyclists and pedestrians are more aware of their surroundings, looking out for fellow travelers rather than assuming that paths will be segregated.

LAND USE PLANNING AND DESIGN

The site contains a few renovated historical buildings and the GWL water tower, which acts as a landmark of the district, surrounded by blocks of high-density housing, designed by five different design teams, but all with a similar color scheme to bring cohesion to the development. One elongated, 610-foot-long, high-rise apartment building with nine stories runs along Waterpootweg Street, the western border of the development (see Figure 2.1). Another elongated apartment complex runs along the north and northwestern borders of the site. This building structure helps to create enclosed areas within the development without applying gates or barriers between GWL Terrein and other neighborhoods. To the east, GWL Terrein is open and pathways connect the development to the nineteenth-century neighborhoods. Overall, 17 apartment buildings are located on-site. As many dwellings as possible have an entrance at street level and access to either a private ground floor garden, a rooftop garden or an open terrace. Incorporated into these residential buildings are ground floor commercial uses, live/work units, housing for persons with mental disabilities, senior housing and wheelchair-accessible housing.

2: AMSTERDAM: GWL TERREIN CASE STUDY

Photo 2.7

Shared garden in GWL Terrein

Source: Photo by Giesbert Nijhuis

Photo 2.8

Wheelchair-accessible residential unit in GWL Terrein

2: AMSTERDAM: GWL TERREIN CASE STUDY

Photo 2.9

Cafe Amsterdam in GWL Terrein

Most of the apartments have three or four rooms, with an average of 3.44 rooms per home. This is higher than the average for the Westerpark District of 2.64 rooms per home. The average home value is also higher in GWL Terrein. In 2005, the average home value in GWL Terrein was $280,000 versus $190,000 for the Westerpark District. The larger size of residential units and higher-quality housing are attractive features for families. Furthermore, 55 percent of residential units are owner-occupied and 45 percent are renter-occupied. Of the rented units, 60 percent are social housing.

Several other uses are also located on the site, such as the Westerpark Community Center. The water company's pumping station was restored and the old engine room is now home to Cafe Amsterdam, a popular restaurant that attracts many visitors to the district. The remaining space in the historic pumping station was converted to offices and a gym. Overall, 50 businesses are located at GWL Terrein (many of them home businesses), employing more than 200 people (www.gwl-terrein.nl/?english). The mix of uses provides residents with shopping, entertainment and employment options within their own neighborhood. In addition, several grocery stores, shops, pharmacies and cafes are located in the surrounding neighborhoods so that residents do not have to go far to run their daily errands, which can easily be done by bicycle or walking.

Photo 2.10

Tram at Van Hallstraat Station near GWL Terrein

Public transportation

GWL Terrein is well served by public transportation. Tram line 10 was extended and terminates just outside the development at the Van Halstraat station. The tram lanes are segregated from car traffic lanes, which helps to increase tram speeds. The tram runs at 10-minute intervals. In addition, bus line 21 provides service from the development to Central Station every 10 minutes.

A variety of transit ticket types are available for the City of Amsterdam. Public transportation users can buy a one-hour ticket, or daily tickets, good for unlimited travel within Amsterdam by tram, bus or metro. Seasonal passes are also available, including weekly, monthly and annual passes. The fares for these passes are zone-based and discounts are available for youth and seniors. All ticket types and passes can be loaded onto the OV-chipkaart, a contactless smartcard that must be swiped upon entering and exiting the public transit vehicle or station. In addition, smartcard users may choose to pay based on the distance they travel. The OV-chipkaart can be used on all public transportation throughout the Netherlands, although fares may vary depending on the region (www.gvb.nl).

Parking

In accordance with GWL Terrein's emphasis on reduced car ownership, parking for the development is extremely limited. None of the residential units have parking spaces on-site. 129 on-street parking spaces are located on the west side of the district, five of which are reserved for carsharing vehicles and two for persons with disabilities. The remaining 122 spaces, equating to 0.2 spaces per residential unit, are part of the city's public parking supply and are therefore first come, first served. The spaces are metered and the cost for visitor parking is about $4 per hour (versus $6 per hour for on-street parking in central Amsterdam). Residential parking permits for these spaces cost about $26 per month, which is much cheaper than hourly parking; however, these permits are extremely limited. Only 110 parking permits, representing 18 percent of households, are available for GWL Terrein residents, and those on the wait

2: AMSTERDAM: GWL TERREIN CASE STUDY

Photo 2.11

Greenwheels carsharing vehicle near GWL Terrein

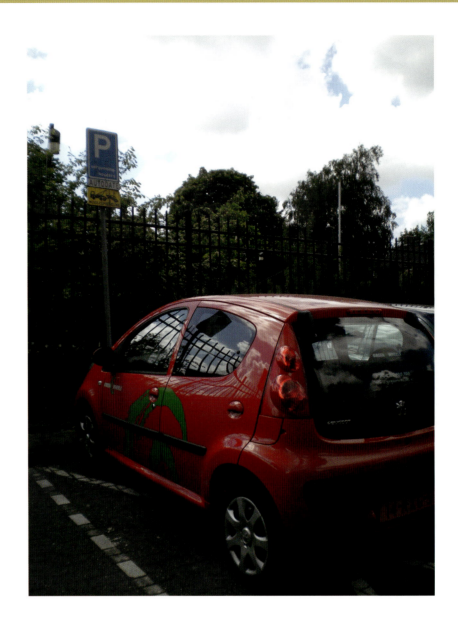

list may wait up to seven years for a permit. Residents of GWL Terrein do not qualify for residential parking permits in the nearby neighborhoods, but some residents have been known to "borrow" parking permits in order to park their cars in the surrounding areas (www.gwl-terrein.nl/?english). A 480-space parking garage is located nearby, which charges $4 per hour for parking up to a maximum of $35 per day. A variety of parking subscriptions are also available, which range from $100 to $325 per month (www.q-park.nl/nl/parkeren-bij-q-park/per-stad/amsterdam/westergasfabriek).

Carsharing

Five carsharing vehicles are located in the parking spaces on the border of the development, belonging to two carsharing organizations: Greenwheels and Diks. Since one of the main goals of the development is to reduce car ownership, provision of carsharing is important to give residents access to a car without having to own one. The vehicles are very popular among residents. Over a quarter of households have a carsharing membership (ITDP 2010). Additionally, Car2Go operates within the City of Amsterdam. This is an innovative, one-way version of carsharing (see Box 2.2).

> **BOX 2.2 ONE-WAY CARSHARING**
>
> In the past few years, a new form of carsharing has emerged, referred to as "one-way" or "flexible" carsharing. Unlike traditional carsharing, vehicles may be returned to other locations than where they were picked up, providing greater flexibility for the user. The parking for these one-way systems is different. The typical model is to allow vehicles to "float", in other words to be parked in any legal parking space within the service area (including at parking meters, with the company paying the parking fee directly to the city). In some models, vehicles can be returned to any designated parking location—typically in on-street parking bays, some with electric vehicle charging ports or in parking garages.
>
> Vehicles are found via a smartphone app that shows the location of parked vehicles in real time and allows the user to make a short "hold" on a vehicle in order to be able to walk to it. Unlike traditional carsharing, one-way services typically do not allow advance reservations since the vehicles are in constant use. It is the operator's challenge to keep the vehicles distributed so that users throughout the city can find a vehicle nearby when they want one. Usage of one-way vehicles is typically charged by the minute, with discounted hourly and even daily rates for longer trips.
>
> Because the one-way carsharing model is so recent, research on the transportation impacts of these services is quite preliminary. Given the flexible nature of trips that these services allow, the transportation and social benefits of one-way carsharing are not as strong as traditional "round trip" carsharing, but are nevertheless present and appear to provide a stepping stone toward lower rates of car ownership and car usage, leading toward car-lite and car-free lifestyles.
>
> The best known providers of one-way carsharing are Daimler's Car2Go (using Smart cars, offered in almost 30 cities in Europe and North America, including two cities with electric fleets), BMW's DriveNow (in six cities in Europe and San Francisco) and Bolloré Blue carsharing (using their proprietary electric Bluecar, called Autolib' in Paris).
>
> Dave Brook, Carsharing Consultant, Team Red US
> www.team-red.us

Car-free declaration

Initial proponents of the development had hoped to actually ban car ownership among residents, but this was not allowed. As an alternative, Ecoplan asked the initial residents of GWL Terrein to sign a non-obligatory declaration of support for the car-free nature of the site. This declaration did not require residents to live car-free, but provided them with information about the intentions of the development. The declaration reminded residents that GWL Terrein is different from other neighborhoods. Parking in the area is difficult for a reason and sustainable forms of transportation are encouraged. Furthermore, the declaration attempted to provide residents with an enhanced feeling of community and the idea that they were involved in a unique experiment in sustainable living. However, today, new residents do not go through Ecoplan. New renters are selected either by one of the five housing associations, which typically do not require a car-free declaration to be signed, or by current owners, who may freely sell their property to anyone they choose. For this reason, the umbrella organization Koepelvereniging has developed a document for new residents, explaining the goals and concepts of the project. The organization is also available to offer advice related to sustainability and car-free living. Therefore, while new residents are no longer asked to state that they agree with the ideals of the project, they are still made aware of the project's original intentions.

Umbrella organization

The umbrella organization Koepelvereniging was created in 1996 to promote the sustainability focus under which the site was developed and to encourage community cohesion. The organization is funded through small fees from residents and the housing associations. Today, Koepelvereniging is the one body that unifies the entire development. The organization has a website and a newsletter for residents, and holds about six meetings per year to discuss community issues such as safety, maintenance and community events. The organization also employs a concierge, who is available on-site to answer questions from residents, performs minor repairs and enforces the car-free restriction (including keeping delivery vehicles from entering the development). Residents are very involved in the organization and help to plan community events, such as an annual soccer tournament held each June, followed by a community dinner (www.gwl-terrein.nl/?english). These efforts help to give residents a sense of community and enhanced focus on the environmental goals of the development.

SUSTAINABLE USE OF RESOURCES

Conservation of resources, water and energy were important components in the initial design of the development. The developers of GWL Terrein experimented with several new techniques. Some worked better than others. The dwellings were built according to the energy performance norm (EPN) of 750 m^3 (natural gas equivalent) per year, which offers considerable energy savings above the standard at the time of 1,400 m^3. However, today the EPN used in GWL Terrein is quite normal for new homes in the Netherlands.

Energy-saving features incorporated in the building design include insulation in the walls, floor and roofs, use of passive solar energy, and cogeneration (combined heat and power, CHP). The site has its own CHP station that supplies hot water to houses and was expected to reduce CO_2 discharge by nearly 50 percent. However, the CHP system has not produced the energy savings originally expected; a large amount of heat energy is lost due to the distance between the heat exchanger and homes. Although energy use of GWL Terrein homes is not considered bad, today the site is not seen as a leading example of energy-saving building features.

Water was to be conserved through using rainwater in toilets. This feature has since been discontinued in most buildings due to maintenance problems.

One successful new feature has to do with the development's waste system. The site was the first in Amsterdam to use an innovative waste disposal system in which waste is separated and collected in subterranean containers at the perimeter of the site, eliminating the need for collection trucks to enter the car-free interior. This system has proven successful at GWL Terrein and was later applied to other neighborhoods of the city (www.gwl-terrein.nl/?english).

QUANTITATIVE ANALYSIS

GWL Terrein is located in one of the world's leading bicycling cities. The city of Amsterdam itself has implemented many policies to encourage bicycling and walking and to reduce car use, such as improved bicycle infrastructure, more bicycle parking facilities, increased police enforcement to prevent bicycle theft, increased bicycle use education to increase bicycle safety, reduced speed limits to improve safety and increased parking prices to reduce car use (Daniel van Motman, pers. comm.). However, efforts at GWL Terrein go even further to encourage non-motorized means of transportation and reduce car

2: AMSTERDAM: GWL TERREIN CASE STUDY

Photo 2.12

Subterranean waste containers in GWL Terrein

Table 2.1 Statistics for GWL Terrein, Amsterdam West and Amsterdam

	GWL Terrein	Amsterdam West	Amsterdam
Population	1,400	77,510	757,000
Area (acres)	15	2,450	54,400
Population density (persons/acre)	95	32	14
Number of residential units	600	N/A	390,000
Cars per 1,000 residents	190	310	370
Bikes per 1,000 residents	1,300	N/A	730
Car parking spaces/residential unit	0.20	N/A	0.72
Mode share for all trips			
Car	6%	20%	28%
Public transit	14%	18%	18%
Bicycle	50%	32%	29%
Walking	30%	30%	25%

Sources: City of Amsterdam, ITDP (2010)

dependency. These efforts have had positive effects on mode share and carbon footprint of residents. A comparison of statistics for GWL Terrein, Amsterdam West and the City of Amsterdam can be seen in Table 2.1.

Density

GWL Terrein is about three times as dense as Amsterdam West, the district in which it is located, and more than five times as dense as the City of Amsterdam. It is even more dense than what is required

2: AMSTERDAM: GWL TERREIN CASE STUDY

Figure 2.2

Mode split for all trips for GWL Terrein, Amsterdam West and Amsterdam residents

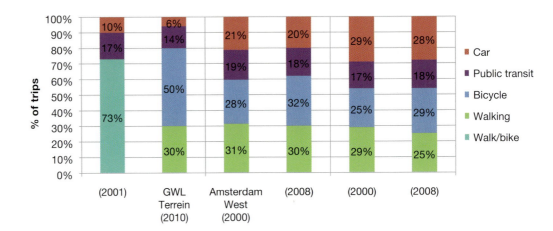

for new growth, or Vinex, locations in the Netherlands (see Box 8.3). Vinex locations are required to have at least 30 homes per hectare, while GWL Terrein has 100 homes per hectare. Higher densities enable more efficient use of resources, which can contribute to reductions in carbon footprint.

Parking

Parking at GWL Terrein is extremely limited. Only 0.20 spaces are provided per residential unit. Although the City of Amsterdam has less than one parking space per residential unit, its 0.72 spaces per unit is still much higher than GWL Terrein. Reducing the availability of parking spaces contributes to a reduced car ownership rate.

Car and bicycle ownership rates

A survey in 2001 found that there were 172 cars per 1,000 residents in GWL Terrein (Scheurer 2001). A more recent, Internet-based survey of GWL Terrein residents conducted by ITDP in 2010 found that this number is slightly higher today at 190 cars per 1,000 residents (ITDP 2010), which is much less than the 310 cars per 1,000 residents in Amsterdam West and about half of the 370 cars per 1,000 residents of Amsterdam (City of Amsterdam). Furthermore, 15 percent of households surveyed gave up a car after moving to GWL Terrein. The number of bicycles owned per resident has not changed significantly. The 2001 survey found 1,346 bicycles per 1,000 residents, while the current survey found 1,300 bicycles per 1,000 residents. Indeed, nearly half of all respondents said that there were more than three bicycles owned by their household, and only 2 percent of respondents said that their household had no bikes (ITDP 2010).

Mode share

Auto and bicycle ownership rates have a great effect on the mode of transportation residents use. The survey found that half of all trips taken by GWL Terrein residents are made by bike and 30 percent are made on foot, while only 6 percent are made by car (Figure 2.2). The share of bike trips in GWL Terrein (50 percent) is much higher than that for Amsterdam West (32 percent) and Amsterdam (29 percent). Furthermore, a far smaller share of trips are made by car in GWL Terrein (6 percent) than in West Amsterdam (20 percent) or Amsterdam (28 percent). The total share of non-motorized trips has increased slightly in Amsterdam West between 2000 and 2008 (from 59 percent to 62 percent). The share of non-motorized trips has not changed in the City of Amsterdam (54 percent) during the same time span; however, 4 percent of trips have shifted from walking to cycling. By contrast, the share of non-motorized trips in GWL Terrein has increased by 7 percent between 2001 and 2010 (from 73 percent to 80 percent).

It is also interesting to compare the mode split for different types of trips. In GWL Terrein, 63 percent of residents travel to work by bike versus 32 percent for Amsterdam (Figure 2.3). Likewise, a smaller

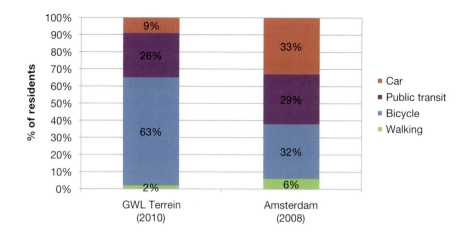

Figure 2.3

Work mode split for GWL Terrein and Amsterdam residents

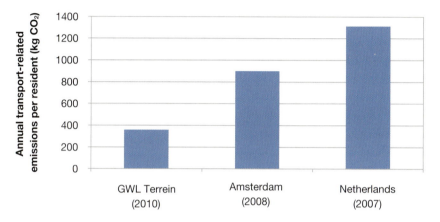

Figure 2.4

Comparison of transport-related emissions for residents of GWL Terrein, Amsterdam and the Netherlands

percentage of GWL Terrein residents travel to work by car (9 percent) than Amsterdam residents (33 percent). Furthermore, 94 percent of GWL Terrein survey respondents said that they do their grocery shopping by bike, 85 percent conduct other shopping by bike, 93 percent run service-related errands (banking, doctor visits, etc.) by bike and 94 percent visit family and friends in Amsterdam by bike (ITDP 2010). These statistics overwhelmingly show that bicycling is the main mode of transport for residents of GWL Terrein.

While the mode share of public transportation is no higher among GWL Terrein residents than Amsterdam residents, GWL Terrein residents still consider it an important option, and most residents use public transit at least once per week. In 2001, it was found that 39 percent of residents had some sort of periodic public transit pass, although the type of pass varied (Scheurer 2001). The 2010 survey found that this number had increased to 46 percent of residents (ITDP 2010). This is even higher than for the City of Amsterdam, where 19 percent of residents have a periodic transit pass (City of Amsterdam).

Distance traveled and emissions

Reduced travel distances also contribute to a reduced carbon footprint. GWL's location gives residents easy access to the city center, where many jobs are located. Indeed, 44 percent of residents travel less than three miles to work, and only 12 percent travel 25 miles or more. Additionally, more than three-fourths of residents travel less than half a mile to get to their grocery store (ITDP 2010). Having close access to destinations such as work and grocery stores encourages travel by bike and walking and reduces miles driven. Therefore, it is not surprising that transport-related emissions of GWL Terrein residents are more than half that of an average Amsterdam resident and one-third that of an average resident of the Netherlands, as seen in Figure 2.4. These estimates are based on annual miles traveled by residents by private and public transportation (for the year indicated), as well as estimates of emissions rates of these vehicles.

2: AMSTERDAM: GWL TERREIN CASE STUDY

Figure 2.5

Importance of various factors on GWL Terrein resident decision not to own a car

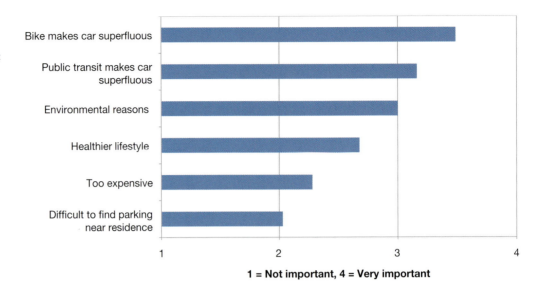

LESSONS LEARNED

All things considered, GWL Terrein works. It allows a diverse array of people to live close to the city center without a car. GWL Terrein includes many features that make it unique among neighborhoods in Amsterdam and encourages sustainable living. However, it is important to acknowledge that the surrounding area and city have a strong impact on the travel behavior of its residents. The extensive network of bicycle paths and efficient public transportation system in the City of Amsterdam allow residents of GWL Terrein to easily travel to other parts of the city using these modes. When non-car owners were asked to rank the importance of different factors in their decision not to own a car, residents gave higher importance ratings to measures such as ease of bicycle and public transit use and lower importance ratings to measures such as expense of owning a car and limited parking (see Figure 2.5). Also, GWL Terrein's location close to the city center has an effect on travel distances of residents. Therefore, it would appear that a new development project in a city with a focus on sustainable transportation, especially located near the center of the city, could have more potential for success than one located in a car-focused city or far from the city center.

Furthermore, Koepelvereniging, the residents' umbrella organization, seems to be an important catalyst for maintaining resident focus on sustainability, reduced car use and social interaction. It also gives residents a common source to turn to with questions or concerns about the development. Such an organization is recommended for other sites planning to implement a sustainability-focused community.

GWL Terrein stands out as the most car-free development we have studied. It represents what we aspire to in creating low carbon communities. It also represents the smallest development studied, begging the question: can this model be replicated on a larger scale? The next case study, Vauban, provides a larger example, and a similar success story, located in Freiburg, Germany.

REFERENCES

Communication with Corine Marseille, Koepelvereniging organization, May 2010.
Communication with Daniel van Motman, Department of Traffic Infrastructure and Transport, City of Amsterdam, May 2010.
Communication with Diego Pos, Koepelvereniging organization, June 2015.
Communication with Hans Niepoth, City of Amsterdam, June 2010.
ITDP (2010) Internet-based survey of GWL Terrein residents.
Scheurer, J. (2001) *Urban Ecology, Innovations in Housing Policy and the Future of Cities: Towards Sustainability in Neighbourhood Communities*, Thesis, Murdoch University, Perth, Western, Australia.

3

Freiburg

Vauban case study

BACKGROUND

Vauban is a well-known car-free district in the City of Freiburg, located in the foothills of the Black Forest in eastern Germany. Vauban was highlighted extensively in *Green Urbanism* by Timothy Beatley in the late 1990s and was reintroduced into the urban planning literature by Andrea Broaddus and Robert Cervero in 2010 (Broaddus 2010; Cervero and Sullivan 2010). Vauban was built at a time when there was political momentum to develop. The local culture was amicable to supporting car-lite living, and rethinking the role of cars in cities (coincidentally, a similar movement was taking place in San Francisco at the time). The City of Freiburg itself has a history of supporting progressive environmental policies. In 2012, Freiburg was the first city to be awarded the German Sustainability Award, recognizing it as the most sustainable city in Germany. Reasons for this award include the city's focus on environmental policy, solar technology, sustainability and climate protection, which have become driving forces for the economy and urban development. The district of Vauban is a celebrated example of these policies in action. It is a brownfield redevelopment with 2,470 households. The mobility and livability objectives for the district prioritize non-motorized modes of travel. A unique feature of Vauban is that its streets are parking-free, providing more space for citizens to walk and bike without obstacles. Driving on neighborhood streets is limited to picking up and dropping off. Parking is limited and spatially separated from housing.

The ambitious environmental policies implemented in Vauban were also influenced by strong local advocacy and a commitment by citizens to create a sustainable urban development. Potential residents worked with developers to design homes. The result is a diverse, colorful mix of buildings and a strong sense of community. Sustainable use of resources is a focus throughout the development. Buildings are energy efficient, using high standards of thermal insulation, solar energy and renewable woodchip district heating. In addition, citizens pushed for strict restrictions to car use in the district, which helped to facilitate the implementation of many innovative policy and design measures, which has made Vauban a model of sustainable mobility.

PLANNING PROCESS

In 1992, the City of Freiburg initiated a masterplanning competition for a new mixed-use eco-suburb. A 175-acre brownfield redevelopment, located on the western side of the city, opened up this opportunity for development. The resulting district, Rieselfeld, implemented innovative design features such as traffic-calmed streets, no through traffic and a new tram line, which opened in 1997.

Coincidentally, in 1992, the French army vacated a 100-acre site south of the city center. The City of Freiburg initially intended to apply the same model coming out of the masterplanning competition. However, a group of local environmental campaigners formed an association called Forum Vauban, with the objective of introducing more extreme measures into the masterplan. The focus on the measures was to deter car use and create safe streets in which children could play safely. One key feature was the use of U-shaped streets to limit through traffic and thus reduce traffic volumes. A significant regulation implemented in Vauban but not in Rieselfeld was the restriction of no on-street parking in front of homes. This feature alone drastically reduces the number of vehicles present in the neighborhoods, making streets safer and more open.

BOX 3.1
VAUBAN SITE FACTS

Developers:
Multiple, mainly small building cooperatives

Architect:
Kohlhoff & Kohlhoff (masterplan)

Construction began:
1998

Planned completion:
2016

Population:
5,500

Total area:
100 acres

Density:
55 persons/acre

Housing units:
2,470

Jobs on-site:
600

Distance from city center:
2 miles

Parking spaces/residence:
< 0.5

Cars:
172 per 1,000 residents

Non-motorized mode share:
64%

Transit mode share:
19%

Households with carsharing membership:
39%

3: FREIBURG: VAUBAN CASE STUDY

Photo 3.1

Distinctive architecture and car-free streets in Vauban

Source: Photo by Simon Field

> **BOX 3.2 FREIBURG TRANSPORTATION POLICY**
>
> Freiburg's achievements in sustainable transportation since the 1960s include the exclusion of cars from the historic city core; an air quality environmental zone since 2010; reduced city center car parking with fees of up to $3 per hour; extensions of the tram system to Rieselfeld and Vauban; a doubling of local "S-Bahn" train frequencies; rebuilding of the main rail station to include a new transit interchange and a 1,000-space bike storage facility; a dense network of bicycle paths extending more than 250 miles in length; citywide 20 mph or lower speed limits; and "naked junctions" that force drivers to negotiate them at low speed. Freiburgers have elected a Green Mayor since 2002, suggesting strong local eco-awareness and popular support for "green" transportation policies.

The architects Kohlhoff & Kohlhoff of Stuttgart integrated the ideas of Forum Vauban into the masterplan for Vauban, which included information on densities, minimum energy standards and parking regulations. Although a long waiting list of potential residents formed, developers were hesitant to invest in the relatively untested concept. Rather than relying on large developers for funding, Forum Vauban coordinated groups of architects, residents and financers to build cooperatives ("Baugruppen" in German) on small plots purchased by each. Construction began in 1998, and the first two phases were completed by 2004. Most of the original military buildings were demolished; however, three were preserved, the first to create "Haus 37," housing a pub and offices for Forum Vauban and the Association for Car-Free Living, the second as part of a student village, and the third forming a low-cost communal living project.

The Baden Württemberg Land Law in Germany requires that every home have access to a parking space. This kept the development from being completely car-free; however, Forum Vauban worked to ensure that parking available in Vauban is limited, at a parking ratio of less than 0.5 per housing unit. Most parking is separated from residences, located in parking garages on the edge of the district.

3: FREIBURG: VAUBAN CASE STUDY

Photo 3.2

Parking-free street in Vauban

Source: Photo by William Bacon

A legal framework was established through which, by default, residents living on parking-free streets must purchase a parking space in an adjacent parking garage. The Association for Car-Free Living was created to administer this system. The initial cost per space was approximately $18,000 plus a monthly service charge. Residents who do not own a car may sign a legal declaration to this effect and forfeit the parking space and associated costs. However, as part of the arrangement, residents of parking-free streets, who support the car use restrictions, each contributed a fee of approximately $4,000.

Although the residents themselves support the parking-free streets model, the City of Freiburg does not officially support the model. While fewer than 0.5 parking spaces are provided per housing unit, state planning rules regulated that land be set aside for one space per unit in case there was demand for that level of parking eventually. This land is currently being used as public recreational space with a community garden. This provides a reminder that strong community support is often key to introducing such radical initiatives. However, demonstration of their success can help to provide precedence for future developments.

KEY POLICY AND DESIGN MEASURES

Vauban limits car use through parking-free residential streets, spatially and fiscally separated parking and filtered permeability to prevent through traffic. Vauban also features efficient light rail service and high-quality non-motorized transportation infrastructure.

Parking

Parking is a key aspect differentiating Vauban from other districts. The parking ratio in Vauban (spaces per residential unit) is less than 0.5. Parking is provided underground under some residential units, on-street in three specific areas of the development, and in two peripheral parking garages. These two garages have a total of 470 spaces. Most residents live closer to a tram stop than a garage. Residents of parking-free blocks (see Figure 3.1) must either sign a legal contract with the Association for

3: FREIBURG: VAUBAN CASE STUDY

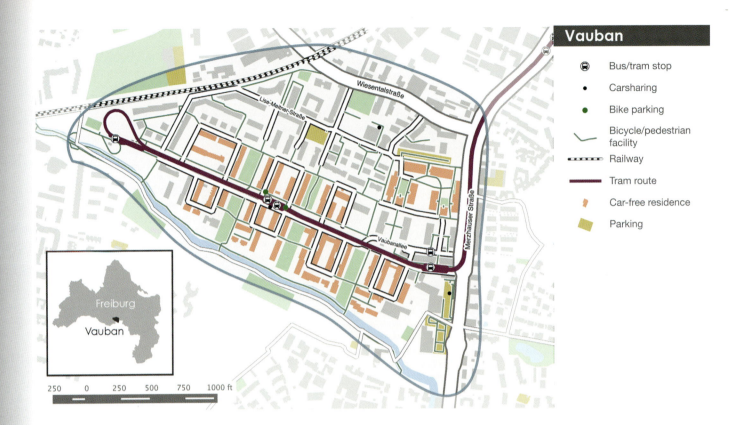

Figure 3.1

Map of Vauban

Source: Map by Amy Smith

Car-Free Living agreeing not to own a car, or purchase a space in one of the two garages for approximately $25,000 plus a monthly maintenance fee (Linck, pers. comm.). Enforcement of the parking-free areas and car ownership declaration are the responsibility of the Association for Car-Free Living. Parking infractions do occur and are not evenly distributed across the district. Some blocks tend to have higher community support for the car-free nature of the district than others.

Public parking is available in some of the garages and 220 metered on-street spaces are available on Vaubanallee. Enforcement of parking and the car-free declaration are the responsibility of the Association for Car-Free Living. Interviews of residents have revealed concern that some residents do own cars despite signing the car-free declaration, in order to avoid paying the steep fee. Legal action is not common, but has been filed against at least two residents known to own a car despite signing the declaration (Sommer and Wiechert 2014).

Urban design

Urban design was an important component in the masterplan of Vauban. Specific street layout, land use and public space design features were incorporated to improve the safety, security and livability of the neighborhood for residents.

Street layout and design

Vaubanallee forms the main spine through the center of the district. Cars may access Vaubanallee from the east, but not from the west, thus preventing through traffic. This ensures that streets in Vauban remain for local access only rather than being used for pass-through traffic, which would be likely to increase traffic volumes and speeds. Tram Route 3 runs along Vaubanallee with three stops.

Several U-shaped residential streets connect to Vaubanallee. These streets are dotted with signs that say "Stellplatzfrei," which means "no parking places." No on-street parking is allowed on these streets, and cars are generally only allowed for pick-up and drop-off purposes. The streets also have

3: FREIBURG: VAUBAN CASE STUDY

Photo 3.3

Signage indicating shared use of street and slow traffic speeds in Vauban

Source: Photo by William Bacon

signs showing children playing alongside a small car icon to indicate that the streets are shared between various users and that vehicles must drive very slowly. Together, the street layout, signage and regulations help to maintain the streets as social spaces where children can play safely and can at times even be seen playing unattended.

LAND USE PLANNING AND DESIGN

Residential buildings in Vauban are 4–5 stories high, and the development has a density of 25 units per acre, including green and other open space. The residential mix includes both renter- and owner-occupied housing and cooperative models, as well as inclusive accommodation projects that promote social integration such as Genova, the Green City Hotel and VAUBANaise. Furthermore, 10 former military barrack buildings were converted into affordable housing by the City of Freiburg Student Union and the SUSI project (self-organized, independent neighborhood initiative) (Quartier Vauban 2014).

Commercial uses and public buildings are located throughout the district, including grocery stores, cafes, restaurants, offices, medical facilities, a community center, nurseries, a pharmacy and a primary school to cover day-to-day needs, as well as innovative projects, such as VillaBan and DIVA, which unite service providers, arts and crafts under one roof. This mix of uses provides opportunities to access jobs, retail, services and cultural opportunities within a short distance.

3: FREIBURG: VAUBAN CASE STUDY

Photo 3.4

Mixed uses: residential buildings with ground floor retail and cafes in Vauban

Source: Photo by Simon Field

Photo 3.5

Pedestrian plaza in Vauban

Source: Photo by William Bacon

PUBLIC SPACE DESIGN

Blocks of green space are located between residential blocks, providing recreational areas and contributing to urban cooling. Communal gardens and walking trails also provide opportunities for recreational activities and reduce the need for residents to travel far distances for such experiences. A public square is used for various community events, including a weekly farmers' market.

28

3: FREIBURG: VAUBAN CASE STUDY

Photo 3.6

Family bicycling in Vauban
Source: Photo by Simon Field

Photo 3.7

Barriers to vehicle entry to pedestrian and bicycle paths in Vauban
Source: Photo by Simon Field

Bicycling and pedestrian infrastructure

Vauban was designed to make travel by walking and bicycling safe and pleasant. The district consists of a dedicated network of streets with limited motorized traffic. Every home has at least one bike parking space—many in secure cellars accessed by ramps. A community bike repair shop offers free labor. The city center and rail station are 12 minutes away by bike.

3: FREIBURG: VAUBAN CASE STUDY

Photo 3.8

Bicycle parking in front of residences in Vauban

Source: Photo by William Bacon

Public transportation

Freiburg's Tram Route 3 was extended into Vauban in 2006. The tram features level boarding, which helps to facilitate ease of boarding. The tram route has three stops along Vaubanallee, and runs on a segregated, green track, which reduces noise and water runoff, in addition to being an attractive right of way. All stops have shelter and display relevant information, including timetables and maps, in addition to real-time electronic displays providing information about the arrival of the next tram. No home is more than 1,500 feet from a tram stop.

Trams arrive every 7.5 minutes, and the route connects to the center of Freiburg in 14 minutes and to the rail station in 18 minutes. Four bus routes also serve the district. Although the tram does not run overnight, buses provide public transportation service at night and on weekends, with approximately one bus per hour. Since 2009, the municipal transit operator has purchased green energy to power the tram system. Furthermore, many of the vehicles use regenerative breaking to return energy to overhead wires. This helps to reduce emissions and energy use of the system.

Public transportation tickets are available at convenience stores, through in-vehicle ticket machines and from tram drivers. Freiburg has developed a reputation for innovative, low-cost ticketing since the introduction of transferable monthly passes in 1984, which led to a doubling of transit patronage in the decade that followed (FitzRoy and Smith 1998). The following ticket types are available in Freiburg:

- City single ticket: $2.40.
- Day pass: $6 (one adult and up to four children) or $12 for up to five adults.
- Transferable monthly pass for the Breisgau Region: $60, or $49 per month as part of an annual subscription.

3: FREIBURG: VAUBAN CASE STUDY

Photo 3.9

Vauban tram on green track
Source: Photo by William Bacon

Photo 3.10

Vauban tram
Source: Photo by Simon Field

The cost of public transportation is affordable compared to driving. RegioKarte holders also get free travel for a second adult on Sundays. Residents in the first parking-free block constructed in Vauban were given a free annual RegioKarte and a national rail discount pass when they moved in.

The Regio-Verkehrsverbund Freiburg (RVF) agency coordinates transit service in the region. The RVF website provides a variety of ticket purchase options, including single-trip and one-day cell phone e-tickets. RVF also offers smartphone apps that provide transit schedule information and route planning.

Carsharing

Thirty dedicated carshare parking spaces are located in Vauban, provided by two carsharing organizations: StadtMobil and Grüne Flotte. Each offers a slightly different pricing structure. StadtMobil charges a deposit of approximately $220 per individual or $330 per household, plus a registration fee of about $20, plus a monthly fee of $0–$16.50 per individual or $0–$22 per household, plus charges of about $1.40–$4.40 per hour, plus $0.25–$0.50 per mile traveled for each trip, depending on the membership package purchased. Packages with a higher monthly fee have lower hourly and distance charges per trip. This allows members to select the most affordable package depending on their use level. Grüne Flotte charges a one-time registration fee of $25 plus $1.60–$4.30 per hour plus $0.30–$0.50 per mile traveled per trip, depending on the vehicle type used (www.stadtmobil-suedbaden.de/start/; www.gruene-flotte-carsharing.de/).

The City of Freiburg also offers a combined transit and carsharing pass called the RegioMobilCard, which offers discounts on a range of mobility services. For an additional $12 per month on an annual subscription, users get:

- carsharing membership for $220 per person and a 20 percent reduction on carshare usage fees;
- 20 percent discount on bike parking and bike rental from the "Mobile" bike center at the rail station; and
- 20 percent off prebooked taxis from Taxi Freiburg.

Having transit and carsharing combined on a mobility pass helps to facilitate use of alternative options to owning a car and improves affordability of these options.

SUSTAINABLE USE OF RESOURCES

Vauban also has a focus on the sustainable use of energy. Low energy standards were set requiring all new buildings be built with at least 65 kWh/m^2. The district also has around 170 passive houses, which have extremely low energy requirements for heating and cooling, resulting in energy consumption of less than 15 kWh/m^2. At least 70 of these passive houses are "plus energy houses," which produce more energy than they use, contributing to the energy grid. These include the Kleehauser zero-energy houses, the PlusEnergy Solar Settlement and Sun Ship, a mixed-use building including housing, workplaces and shops. The district also has a highly efficient cogeneration plant that operates on woodchips and natural gas and contributes to heating the district. Vauban is also one of the largest solar districts in Europe, with more than 500 square meters of solar collectors (Quartier Vauban 2014).

Furthermore, Vauban has many buildings and homes with green roofs, and rainwater collection systems, water from which is reused throughout the district.

Table 3.1 Statistics for Vauban, Rieselfeld and Freiburg

	Vauban	Rieselfeld	Freiburg
Population	5,000	9,000	218,000
Area (acres)	100	175	37,800
Population density (persons/acre)	50	51	5.8
Jobs per resident	0.12	0.09	N/A
Cars per 1,000 residents	172	320	428
Car parking spaces/residential unit	< 0.5	1.2	N/A
Mode share for all trips			
Car	16%	30%	30%
Transit	19%*	25%	18%
Bicycle/walking	64%	45%	52%

* Prior to opening of the tram extension to Vauban

QUANTITATIVE ANALYSIS

Vauban is compared to the reference district of Rieselfeld in order to quantify the benefits of policy and design measures limiting car use. Rieselfeld is larger, but similar in demographics to Vauban. Both are relatively new developments. Initially, Vauban was conceptualized to replicate many features of Rieselfeld, including provision of a mix of uses, "play streets" and high-quality bicycle and pedestrian infrastructure. However, Vauban varied from Rieselfeld by prohibiting parking in certain residential areas and by unbundling parking from the cost of residential units. A survey of residents from these two developments was conducted in May 2002 (Nobis 2003a), and this section mainly draws from results from that survey. It should be noted that the survey was completed after the parking-free blocks were completed, but before the extension of Tram Route 3 into Vauban. Therefore, while these results provide an initial comparison of residents, a new survey could show different results.

Mode share

Car use in Vauban is around half of that recorded in Rieselfeld and the City of Freiburg, with non-motorized transportation accounting for almost two-thirds of all trips (Figure 3.2). Figure 3.3 summarizes commute mode share for Vauban residents and Freiburg residents. Vauban residents were divided between car-free households and car-owning households. This figure in particular demonstrates the key difference in travel behavior among Vauban residents. While across the city of Freiburg as a whole, the bicycle accounted for 34 percent of commute trips, in Vauban, 61 percent of commute trips made by car-owning households and 91 percent of commute trips made by car-free households were by bike.

Figure 3.4 summarizes mode share of Vauban residents for shopping trips and separates car-free households from car-owning households. The majority of residents in both groups conducted daily shopping trips by bike, reflecting the excellent provision of local retail facilities, easily accessible by bike. Even bulk shopping trips, one of the most difficult trip types to shift away from the private car, were primarily made by bike among car-free residents. Among car-owning residents of Vauban, 24 percent conducted bulk shopping trips by bike and 73 percent made these trips by car.

Data for the main mode used for leisure trips are shown in Figure 3.5. Individuals without access to a household car made an impressive 83 percent of such trips by non-motorized means, with significantly greater bicycle use compared to car-owning Vauban residents and all households in Freiburg. Only 2 percent of leisure trips made by residents from car-free households were by car, clearly demonstrating that car ownership is the primary determinant of car use.

3: FREIBURG: VAUBAN CASE STUDY

Figure 3.2

Mode split for all trips for Vauban, Rieselfeld and Freiburg

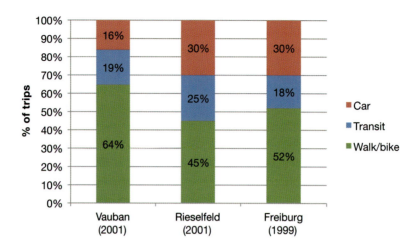

Figure 3.3

Mode split for commute trips for Vauban and Freiburg residents

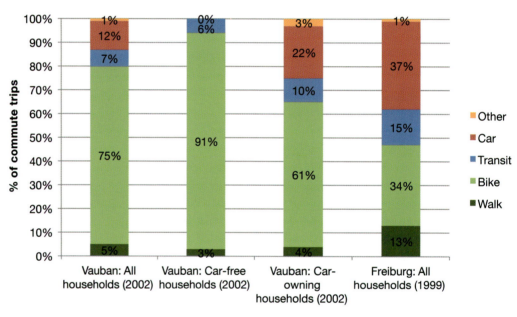

Figure 3.4

Mode split for shopping trips for Vauban residents

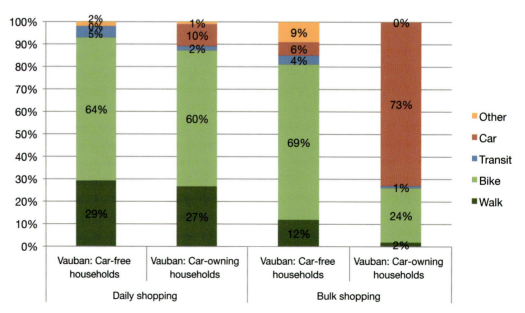

34

3: FREIBURG: VAUBAN CASE STUDY

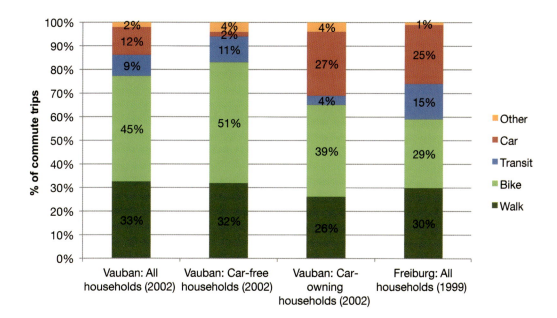

Figure 3.5

Mode split for leisure trips for Vauban and Freiburg residents

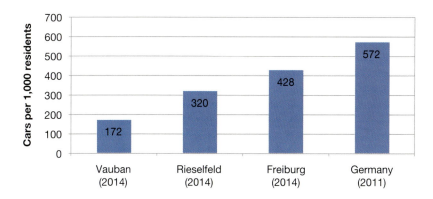

Figure 3.6

Car ownership rates for Vauban, Rieselfeld, Freiburg and Germany

Survey respondents were also asked about their transportation choices before moving to Vauban. Among car owners, 41 percent stated that they used a bicycle more frequently after moving to Vauban than they had before, demonstrating the impact of sustainable transportation policies and design measures on travel behavior. Transit use among Vauban residents was found to be lower than for the city as a whole. However, as mentioned, the survey was conducted prior to the introduction of tram service in 2006. Therefore, it is likely that transit use by Vauban residents has since increased. Potentially, some residents have shifted some non-motorized transportation trips to the tram, particularly in the winter.

Vehicle ownership and carsharing

Considering only the parking-free blocks, approximately 40 percent of Vauban households did not own a car according to the 2002 survey. Figure 3.6 summarizes current car ownership rates for residents of Vauban, Rieselfeld, Freiburg and Germany. Although Vauban has a greater proportion of low-income residents and students than Rieselfeld, which typically have lower car ownership rates, this is offset by having twice as many households with children, a demographic group expected to be more car-reliant. Rieselfeld has succeeded in reducing car ownership to the level of Freiburg's inner districts, but Vauban has almost halved this at 172 cars per 1,000 residents.

In 2002, 39 percent of Vauban households were registered with a carsharing organization. At the time, only 0.1 percent of German drivers were carsharing members. In addition, 70 percent of

3: FREIBURG: VAUBAN CASE STUDY

Photo 3.11

Car-free streets in Vauban

Source: Photo by Simon Field

respondents without a car stated that they used carsharing more often after moving to Vauban than they did before.

There is a question of causality: do residents give up their car as a result of Vauban's parking concept, or has the decision to live car-free been made long before moving in? In answer to this, the Nobis research revealed that 81 percent of the inhabitants of car-free households previously owned a car: 57 percent gave up their car just before moving to Vauban. Interestingly, 65 percent of residents moved to Vauban from elsewhere in Freiburg (www.vauban.de). These statistics suggest that more than half of those without a car were persuaded to do so by the unique combination of policy and design measures offered by the district.

In summary, the inhabitants of Vauban are enthusiastic walkers and bicyclists, but car-owning residents tend to default to the car for awkward trips, such as those involving heavy loads, and are more likely to use the car for longer leisure trips rather than walking or biking.

Transit use

According to the 2002 survey, 56 percent of car-free households in Vauban owned at least one RegioKarte transit pass, compared with 47 percent of car-owning households on parking-free streets and 32 percent of car-owning households in the conventional area. In addition, 72 percent of car-free residents and 49 percent of car-owning residents of Vauban owned a national rail discount card, compared with only 10 percent of residents nationwide (Nobis 2003b). These findings (prior to the opening of the tram extension into Vauban) can be interpreted as an indication of the importance of local transit for day-to-day mobility, and rail as a substitute for the car for medium- to longer-distance journeys.

Residents' views on Vauban

Based on the 2002 survey results, the majority (80 percent) of residents from car-free households felt that organizing their life without owning a car was "easy" or "very easy." This finding can be attributed to the high-quality bike and pedestrian infrastructure, the mix of uses and services, proximity to the city center, good regional transit links and the availability of carsharing. However, 67 percent of car-owning residents in parking-free streets reported being dissatisfied with being unable to park outside their home. Given that almost 60 percent of parking-free households have a car, this implies that approximately 40 percent of residents in the parking-free areas considered Vauban's advantages to outweigh this inconvenience, although they would like to have "the best of both worlds," helping to explain the parking infractions.

LESSONS LEARNED
Vauban is a success story, with greatly reduced car ownership and bicycle substitution of routine car trips as tangible benefits of the policy and design strategies. The local community support for car-free and car-lite development was critical to its genesis. Keys to its success were the economic and spatial decoupling of parking, leading to the reduction of driving as the default mode of transportation. Another critical component was accessibility to goods, services and jobs, making it possible for people to go about their lives without a car. Good accessibility can be facilitated through the provision of local services and jobs, proximity to the city center, extensive bicycle and pedestrian infrastructure, and efficient, low-cost regional transit services. Application of these strategies can enable developments such as Vauban to attract people not predisposed to an altruistic car-free lifestyle, as is evidenced by the finding that 57 percent of residents in car-free households gave up their car when they moved to Vauban.

Parking
Transferability of the economically and spatially decoupled parking model into other new developments is possible, although this is unlikely to be accepted in the absence of complementary measures enabling a shift to other modes. Vauban has demonstrated that legal barriers such as minimum parking standards can be overcome. Implementation of parking maximums and requirements that parking be financially unbundled from both residential and commercial uses is recommended for new developments.

Vauban has had some issues of illegal parking on the parking-free streets, which until now has been largely self-policed by residents applying pressure on their neighbors. Formal warnings should be issued to offenders in the first instance, to avoid possible future tensions between residents. Legal action may be required against the small subset of car-owning residents who claim to live car-free and therefore evade parking fees. Lessons for future developments attempting to apply the model of spatially separating parking from residences should ensure that formal enforcement mechanisms are in place from the beginning to deter noncompliance with set parking policies.

Masterplanning
Masterplanning competitions have been successful in Vauban and other developments, working to meet sustainability guidelines developed by local and regional planning authorities. The sale of small plots of publicly owned land to several different associations of developers, architects and potential residents ("Baugruppen") is a model that could be replicated elsewhere, helping to mitigate the unpopularity of and lack of a sense of community in unappealing, anonymous estates of identical homes.

Public transportation

One criticism of Vauban is that the tram extension had not opened by the time most residents had moved in, a factor that could have contributed to greater car ownership and the desire of developers to build later blocks with bundled parking. Oftentimes, travel patterns are established when first moving to a new location. Introduction of the tram after residents had established a routine that did not involve public transit may have made it less likely that they would shift to using the tram once it was available. For other developments, it is important to ensure that high-quality transit is in place before the development is complete, to ensure that residents can avail themselves of this option from the outset.

Transportation demand management

The dissatisfaction among some car-owning residents regarding parking could be ameliorated through a transportation demand management program that includes personalized travel planning, including advice on how to navigate the transit system, incorporate walking and biking into daily routines (including for shopping), and how to plan leisure trips without a car. Greater marketing for the RegioMobilCard could be worthwhile, building on the awareness-raising effect of the free annual RegioKarte issued to residents of parking-free households upon moving in. New developments similarly should consider providing programs and incentives to raise awareness of alternative travel options, such as discounted prices on transit passes, carshare memberships and bike-share memberships, as well as personal travel advice programs.

CONCLUSION

Both the GWL Terrain and Vauban case studies show us that a local political culture predisposed to building without cars is unique but growing. Both developments had citizenry enthusiastic about creating car-free communities. In our next case study, we see that even in the United States, there is demand for car-free and car-lite developments, demonstrating the growing momentum for low carbon communities and lifestyles.

REFERENCES

Beatley, T. (2000) *Green Urbanism: Learning from European Cities*, Washington, DC: Island Press.
Broaddus, A. (2010) *A Tale of Two Eco-Suburbs in Freiburg, Germany: Parking Provision and Car Use*, Paper presented at TRB 2010 Annual Meeting.
Car-Sharing Südbaden—Freiburg: www.car-sharing-freiburg.org/goto/kosten/.
Cervero, R. and Sullivan, C. (2010) *Toward Green TODs*, Working Paper UCB-ITS-VWP-2010-7, UC Berkeley Center for Future Urban Transport, Berkeley, CA.
EC (2010) *Energy and Transport in Figures 2010*, European Commission, Luxembourg.
FitzRoy, F. and Smith, I. (1998) "Public transport demand in Freiburg: why did patronage double in a decade?" *Transport Policy*, 5: 163–173.
Freiburg GreenCity: www.fwtm.freiburg.de/servlet/PB/menu/1174649_l1/index.html.
"Green City Freiburg" (2014) City of Freiburg: www.freiburg.de/pb/site/Freiburg/get/742991/Green-City-Brochure_English.pdf.
Linck, H. (2010) Personal communication with Hannes Linck (Verein für autofreies Wohnen e.v.) in September 2010.

Melia, S. (2006) *On the Road to Sustainability: Transport and Carfree Living in Freiburg*, University of the West of England.

Nobis, C. (2003a) *Bewohnerbefragung Vauban: Bericht im Rahmen des Projektes "Umsetzungsbegleitung des Verkehrskonzeptes im Stadtteil Freiburg-Vauban,"* Berlin: Deutsches Zentrum für Luftund Raumfahrt e.V.

Nobis, C. (2003b) "The impact of car-free housing districts on mobility behaviour: case study," in E. Beriatos, C. A. Brebbia, H. Coccossis and A. Kungolos (eds), *Conference on Sustainable Planning and Development*, Dorset: WIT, pp. 701–720.

"Quartier Vauban" (2014) City of Freiburg: www.freiburg.de/pb/site/Freiburg/get/647919/Infotafeln_Vauban_en.pdf.

R+T (1999) Verkehrsentwicklungsplan Freiburg. Teil A: Problemanalyse, Freiburg: R+T.

Scheurer, J. (2001) *Urban Ecology, Innovations in Housing Policy and the Future of Cities: Towards Sustainability in Neighbourhood Communities*, Perth: Murdoch University Institute of Sustainable Transport.

Sommer, U. and Wiechert, C. (2014) "Lernen von Vauban. Ein Studienprojekt und mehr," Architecture Department, RWTH Aachen University, Aachen, Germany.

Umweltbundesamt (2009) *Daten zum Verkehr. Ausgabe 2009*, Umweltbundesamt, Dessau-Roßlau.

URBED: www.urbed.com/.

VAG Freiburg (municipal transit operator): www.vag-freiburg.de/.

4
San Francisco
Market and Octavia case study

> **BOX 4.1**
> **MARKET AND OCTAVIA SITE FACTS**
>
> *Developer:*
> Multiple
>
> *Architect:*
> Multiple
>
> *Population:*
> 30,800
>
> *Projected population:*
> 36,500
>
> *Total area:*
> 740 acres
>
> *Current density:*
> 42 persons/acre
>
> *Projected density:*
> 49 persons/acre
>
> *Current residential units:*
> 19,100
>
> *Projected residential units:*
> 22,600
>
> *Planned completion:*
> 2025
>
> *Distance from city center:*
> 1.5 miles
>
> *Cars:*
> 400 cars/1,000 residents
>
> *Percentage of households that are car-free:*
> 44%
>
> *Non-motorized commute mode share:*
> 16%
>
> *Public transit commute mode share:*
> 44%

INTRODUCTION

In the United States, a national policy to reduce transportation greenhouse gas (GHG) emissions has mostly faltered, leaving cities and states to mitigate global warming on their own. And while car-free and car-lite developments have not been the norm, in the last decade a handful of cities, such as Portland, Seattle and San Francisco, have taken important steps toward addressing GHGs by enabling new residential and commercial development that reduces car dependency. Because our aim in this book is to encourage and inspire North American city planners and urban advocates, a longer, more detailed U.S. case study is warranted and shows that even here, new thinking has emerged and been deployed. In San Francisco, planners, neighborhood residents and sustainable transportation advocates collaborated to rezone several sections of the city to encourage transit-oriented infill development and relaxed rules requiring car parking for new homes. This included elimination of minimum parking requirements so that housing can be potentially car-free, and design guidelines that restrict garage facades and other street-level barriers to walkability, and which help in creating vibrant street life.

This chapter profiles one section of San Francisco, known as the Market and Octavia area, which was one of the first substantial low carbon rezonings in a residential section of San Francisco and a bellwether for similar smart growth and transit-oriented development plans in the Bay Area, California and throughout the United States. The Market and Octavia Plan combines progressive visions of promoting car-lite development with real estate ambitions for urban infill and re-urbanization. The name of the area reflects the intersection of Market Street with Octavia Boulevard, an intersection once crossed by the elevated Central Freeway (Figure 4.1). Formally adopted in 2009, the centrally located Market and Octavia Plan area abuts San Francisco's Civic Center, within a short walking distance to more than 50,000 well-paying jobs. The downtown San Francisco Financial District is 1.5 miles east of the Market and Octavia Plan area.

The Market and Octavia area is also a major regional destination because of multiple performing arts venues adjacent or within the area, including the San Francisco Symphony, Opera, Ballet, and Jazz Center. As of late 2014, over 1,500 new units of housing have been constructed in the plan area since 2008 (SFPD 2015). Another 3,500 new units are under construction or in the planning stage, with a total of 5,500 to 6,000 infill units allowed in the plan area. To date, the cumulative off-street parking ratio for newly completed and future housing is roughly between 0.5 and 0.6 parking spaces per residential unit (Millard-Ball 2015). In addition, 3,000 new jobs are projected for the area, also with little to no off-street parking expected.

BACKGROUND

The eastern third of the Market and Octavia area burned to the ground after the infamous 1906 earthquake and firestorm, and so was rebuilt in the following decade with modest accommodation of automobiles. Although mostly residential today, the area was once a light industrial district interspersed with apartments, surface parking lots and the elevated, double-deck Central Freeway, which bifurcated the area in 1959.

4: SAN FRANCISCO: MARKET & OCTAVIA CASE STUDY

Figure 4.1

Map of Market and Octavia

Source: Map by Amy Smith

The western two-thirds of the Market and Octavia area includes portions of Hayes Valley, Duboce Triangle and Mission Dolores, which are compact, moderately dense mixed-income and mixed-use neighborhoods located in San Francisco's "Victorian Belt," a collection of historic neighborhoods ringing downtown San Francisco built between the 1870s and 1900. This area was spared from the fires following the 1906 earthquake and is well preserved. There is an abundance of two- and three-story row houses and flats on small lots, within fine-grained blocks, many with alleys and most built before automobiles proliferated.

The Market and Octavia area is a viable place to live without a car. Within the plan area, 44 percent of households are car-free (ACS 2006–2010). Although garages have been inserted beneath many homes, much of the housing stock has little to no off-street parking, and is well-served by transit, with high frequency radial bus service on key streets, a streetcar operating above ground on Market Street, light rail operating underground on Market Street, and two Bay Area Rapid Transit (BART) stations—the regional rail transit system—located nearby.

4: SAN FRANCISCO: MARKET & OCTAVIA CASE STUDY

Photo 4.1

View of Octavia Boulevard

Photo 4.2

Aerial view of freeway before removal

Source: Photo by Gordon Peters/San Francisco Chronicle/Polaris

4: SAN FRANCISCO: MARKET & OCTAVIA CASE STUDY

Photo 4.3

View of existing freeway off-ramp onto Market Street and Octavia Boulevard

Notwithstanding the minor hills, the Market and Octavia area is excellent for utilitarian bicycle travel. Starting on Market Street, the "Wiggle" is a bicycle route of citywide importance because it enables one to bike across the city without having to encounter many steep grades. At a relaxed speed of 10 miles per hour, a bicyclist can reach the iconic Ferry building and bay front in 20 minutes, Golden Gate Park in less than 20 minutes and the Mission District in 5 to 10 minutes.

Yet, despite all of these attributes, the Market and Octavia area is also burdened with a substantial share of San Francisco's automobile traffic. Every day, more than 150,000 cars and trucks stream through on Van Ness Avenue and on a handful of multi-lane, one-way arterials called "one-way couplets," as well as the vestigial Central Freeway and Octavia Boulevard. Originally constructed in 1959, the alignment of the Central Freeway paralleled Van Ness Avenue and was intended to link the Golden Gate Bridge to the Bay Bridge and to freeways to the south of the city. However, the planned segment to the north was rejected in the early 1960s during San Francisco's famous freeway revolts. That might have preserved the livability of neighborhoods to the north, but parts of Market and Octavia area were transformed into a bypass for cars and a de facto node in the regional highway system. The juxtaposition of dense housing and a thruway for automobiles was a quandary that neighborhood residents and planners spent decades trying to solve and, as will be discussed below, remains largely unresolved.

The origins of the Market and Octavia Plan are linked to the Central Freeway and the one-way couplets. In 1989, the magnitude 6.9 Loma Prieta Earthquake damaged the portion of the Central Freeway that had been completed 30 years earlier. This provided an opportunity to consider removing the elevated freeway, and thus began a two-decade political debate and planning process that resulted in partial freeway removal in Hayes Valley and the initiation of the Market and Octavia Plan, which was meant to use zoning to stitch the area back together and promote low-car living.

PLANNING PROCESS

Removing the Central Freeway was the first step toward the Market and Octavia Plan but this was an extremely politicized endeavor. In the Hayes Valley neighborhood, a stratum of well-educated, politically progressive middle-class residents organized in support of removal in the mid-1990s. Small businesses along Hayes Street also endorsed removal. As well, a newly invigorated, citywide sustainable transportation discourse, led in part by a vocal bicycle advocacy movement, was gaining traction and by the mid to late 1990s had achieved political parity with other progressive causes. Out of this was born the Hayes Valley Neighborhood Association, which went on to champion the Market and Octavia Plan and watchdog the implementation of the plan.

With combined effort, proponents of freeway removal countered the state's highway department, automotive interests and a group of politically conservative, pro-freeway homeowners on San Francisco's more automobile-oriented west side. In 1997, the latter groups put the decision about the freeway to city voters using San Francisco's petition-driven ballot process. They wanted the freeway rebuilt entirely as before, although with a wider single deck instead of a seismically unsound double deck. To the surprise of many, they were successful, and by late 1997 it seemed that the freeway would be rebuilt.

However, Hayes Valley activists put a second ballot measure to remove the freeway up for vote in 1998. That too passed, sparking confusion about the fate of the freeway. In 1999, a third ballot measure pit rebuilding against removal, with a new landscaped boulevard if the removal side won. In a cliffhanger election year with a high-profile mayor's election, removal advocates won at the ballot, but not without compromise. Though voters approved freeway removal in Hayes Valley, the freeway was to be rebuilt south of Market Street, thus continuing to have a significant impact on the area, channeling high vehicle volumes through the area and shifting land use problems to the South of Market (SoMa) neighborhood. Significantly as well, the financing of the freeway removal and replacement boulevard was directly tied to the sale of 22 newly vacated parcels (amounting to seven acres) where the freeway once ran overhead. The proceeds of land sales would underwrite the new boulevard and other traffic mitigations related to the removal, as Caltrans (the State Highway Department) vehemently opposed removal and refused to finance it.

Meanwhile, the 1999–2000 "dot-com" boom transformed parts of the city into trendy, urbane alternatives to the low-density, homogenous office parks in Silicon Valley. The areas near the former freeway, ironically proximate to the future touchdown ramp South of Market, experienced tremendous pressure for new housing with ample residential off-street parking for Silicon Valley commuters.

The stakes over off-street parking policy were especially high and kick-started the drafting of the Market and Octavia Plan in 2000. In addition to the 22 "freeway parcels," further afield there were many more underutilized parcels, including surface parking lots, gasoline service stations, automobile dealerships and a six-acre former college campus. Cumulatively, this land amounted to the possibility of 6,000 new housing units and 10,000 new residents. Not wishing to engage in a parcel-by-parcel skirmish over parking, city planners, progressive mobility activists, the new Hayes Valley Neighborhood Association, San Francisco Planning and Urban Research (SPUR) (a prominent local developer think tank), considered an area-wide, consensus-based land use plan that would define the parameters of development, including heights, bulk, density and parking.

> **BOX 4.2 PLANNING IN CALIFORNIA**
>
> Planning in California is guided by many forces, including governmental, private, community and individual. Much of this planning takes place at a local level. Local governments use several tools to guide and implement planning. One of the primary tools is the General Plan.
>
> The General Plan is a comprehensive document that consists of broad policy statements outlining goals and objectives for future development of a city. It guides the physical development of a community in that it is the framework that directs local planning decisions.
>
> The General Plan, which is required under Government Code Section 65300, grew out of the state's planning history. In 1937, California was one of the first states in the United States to require cities and counties to adopt Masterplans. In the 1950s, the state began requiring preparation of elements or sections of the Masterplans, of which land use and circulation elements were the first. Fifteen years later, in 1965, California renamed the Masterplan a "General Plan".
>
> General Plan also encompasses "Area Plans," or "Community Plans," which are specific versions of the General Plan devoted to a particular geographic area. Area and Community Plans address a particular region or community within the overall planning area of the General Plan. Area or Community Plans also provide opportunities for understanding and resolving local land use and planning conflicts. Ultimately, an Area or Community Plan must be consistent with the locality's overarching General Plan.
>
> The San Francisco General Plan currently contains the following elements: residence, commerce and industry, recreation and open space, community facilities, transportation, community safety, environmental protection, urban design and arts. Over the past several years, the Planning Department, in collaboration with community stakeholders, has developed and adopted several Area Plans, including the Market and Octavia Area Plan, to encourage neighborhood growth and change, and envision community improvements decades into the future. The Market and Octavia Area Plan details a summary of policies and objectives that are categorized into the following: land use and urban form, housing, building with a sense of place, streets and open spaces, balancing transportation choices, infill development on key sites, and a new neighborhood in SoMa West.
>
> —Andrea Contreras, San Francisco Planning Department

When planning initiated in May 2000, there were approximately 16,300 housing units and 29,000 people living in the plan area (2000 Census). A series of meetings, workshops and a bus tour were hosted by city planners. In late 2002, a draft plan was released for public review, and then underwent environmental review, which is required in California for any proposed change to the physical environment. As the environmental study was underway, the city became embroiled in a legal controversy over traffic engineering metrics that complicated the study, and the city also lacked adequate funding to complete the study in a timely manner. A draft environmental study was released in summer 2005, and throughout 2006 and 2007 the plan was vetted, debated and amended, with substantial debate involving parking policy, affordable housing quotas, historic preservation, density and developer impact fees that would help underwrite infrastructure needs stemming from new residences. Along the way, the Hayes Valley Neighborhood Association, SPUR and other neighborhood allies pressed for the plan to be adopted.[1]

The City Planning Commission approved the plan in 2007 after a series of cantankerous public hearings, but to the dismay of sustainable transportation advocates, diluted progressive parking controls. However, since the adoption of the plan included rezoning and integration into the city legal code, the plan had to next get legislative approval from the San Francisco Board of Supervisors. This led to another year of vetting and debate, which resulted in more progressive parking policies, a slightly higher affordable housing quota (attained through developer impact fees), stronger historic preservation and the zcreation of a citizen advisory committee to advise the city on how to prioritize allocation of impact fees.

In spring 2008, the San Francisco Board of Supervisors formally adopted the plan and the community advisory committee began meeting that summer. All things considered, it took 19 years, from the earthquake in 1989 to final city approval in 2008, to develop the Market and Octavia Plan. By then, the global economic crisis was in full swing, and potential development both citywide and in the plan area was delayed further. Development in the area remained stagnant until 2012, when real estate speculation boomed, particularly in response to a new wave of technology and social media corporations coming to the city, attracting a specific demographic of new residents to the city who were primarily young, well-educated, high-income and embracing of urban living (commonly referred to as "tech" workers).

As of early 2015, there were over 5,000 new housing units either built, under construction or in the pipeline, on or very proximate to the seven acres of land that opened up for redevelopment as a result of the freeway removal. This represents more than a quarter of housing units in the entire Market and Octavia Plan area (SFPD 2015).

Long-term, the Market and Octavia Plan includes calls for a study, in part funded by impact fee revenue, for the dismantling of the remainder of the Central Freeway south of Market Street. This segment of highway is now almost 60 years old and beyond its expected life cycle. If it is to be retrofit, the project would take years, a new deck would have to be constructed and traffic would be aggravated considerably. Activists in Hayes Valley and elsewhere have asked, since there will be a closure for some time, why not simply use this as an opportunity to dismantle the elevated vestigial highway and replace it with an extension of the Octavia Boulevard. Along with significant traffic mitigation, the proposal could also open up more land for housing development.

KEY POLICY AND DESIGN MEASURES

The Market and Octavia Plan was one of the most far-reaching and innovative rezonings to take place in San Francisco in decades. Off-street parking regulations, affordable housing requirements, urban design, public transportation investments and new impact fees were some of the main changes that were expected to help facilitate car-free or car-lite living. Additionally, a community advisory committee made up of local residents and business owners was established to recommend how impact fee revenue would be spent and monitor the plan's implementation.

The language in the Market and Octavia Plan explicitly seeks to reduce automobile dependency. Originally built before the automobile, the existing transit network is targeted for capacity expansion and improved reliability. Since up to 45 percent of households within the plan area did not own automobiles when adopted, the goal is to enhance this metric by seeking to "ensure some continued increment of car-free housing, similar to historic and existing patterns." This goal can be met by eliminating parking minimums and capping the maximums, but it also requires robust transit, coupled with bicycle and pedestrian improvements.

Photo 4.4

SF Jazz

Off-street parking

The Market and Octavia Plan was especially groundbreaking because of its reform of off-street parking, and preliminary estimates suggest that about half of all new housing units in the plan area are accompanied by off-street parking.[2] Under the typical guidelines for residential off-street parking found in San Francisco, dating back to the mid-1950s, housing would be required to have one off-street parking space for each new unit. These parking "minimums," as codified in San Francisco's zoning code, mean that if the 6,000 new units allowed in the plan area were built, 6,000 new parking spaces would be constructed in the Market and Octavia area under the conventional city zoning code. If the new housing were built by mainstream American parking standards (with ratios typically greater than 1:1), more than 10,000 parking spaces would probably be constructed.

The Market and Octavia Plan dispenses with conventional parking standards and eliminates parking minimums, while a range of "maximums" reduce the allowable ratios for parking to lower than one parking space per residential unit. In the areas of the Market and Octavia Plan closest to the downtown, the permitted parking maximum is one space for every four residential units (0.25:1). In the mixed-use neighborhood commercial corridors along Market Street and other transit-served streets, the permitted parking maximum is one space per two residential units (0.5:1), and in the remainder of the plan area the maximum is three parking spaces for every four residential units (0.75:1). Additionally, the plan bans curb cuts for driveways on streets with transit service or identified as neighborhood-serving commercial corridors.

The plan also waived requirements for parking for retail and entertainment establishments, which was especially important for the development of SF Jazz, the largest jazz performance center west of the Mississippi, and for a youth recreation center, both of which were financially viable because parking was not required on-site. And with 3,000 new jobs expected in the plan area, reduced parking ensures fewer car trips by employees into an already oversaturated district of the city.

Moreover, the elimination of parking minimums results in relatively less expensive housing. Housing without parking costs less to build, something especially important when subterranean excavation and seismic engineering are required, and this presumably discounts housing costs for future residents. The plan requires the cost of parking, if provided, to be decoupled from rents or sale prices of housing units (typically referred to as "unbundling" parking), ensuring that renters and buyers have transparency in the cost of car ownership, and protecting car-free households from unfairly subsidizing car owners, as is the case throughout most of America's housing market. The plan also allows small "in-law" units, often tucked beneath or behind older homes. These units would not be possible with the conventional 1:1 parking minimums, and providing them can help address the city's affordable housing by enabling housing for smaller households or expanding households with relatives needing to live nearby.

Lastly, the Market and Octavia Plan's parking policies recognize that if people have easy access to cars and parking, they will tend to shop elsewhere, making local, walkable retail less viable and potentially shifting retail dollars out of the community.

On-street parking

While the Market and Octavia Plan is celebrated for its innovative off-street parking policies, the plan also has language encouraging the reform and modernization of on-street, or curbside, parking. It should be noted that the jurisdiction over the curb is not the Planning Department, but rather the San Francisco Municipal Transportation Agency (SFMTA), and so a different decision-making process determines street parking policy. Nonetheless, there are two key parking reforms called for in the plan—reforming residential permit parking (RPP) and establishing demand-responsive variable pricing for parking in the commercial districts such as Hayes Valley and Upper Market. Unlike the reforms of off-street parking, RPP and parking pricing have lagged.

In terms of residential permit parking, streets in much of the Market and Octavia area are part of an RPP zone that was established in the 1970s, and that spans across a wide geography in the center of San Francisco. It was designed primarily to discourage suburban motorists from parking in the neighborhood and commuting to downtown by transit. Today, the residential parking zone is fragmented and priced too low, and new innovations in parking management could be implemented.

One such innovation is "SF Park," which is a demand-based variable pricing scheme focused on commercial districts (see SFPark.com). Motorists use smartphone apps to identify available parking spaces and to pay for parking. Curbside parking prices are determined by analysis of demand, so that high-demand spots are priced higher, while lower demand brings lower prices. SF Park replaced the city's existing metered zones, and so was established in the eastern part of the Market and Octavia area as part of a citywide deployment.

4: SAN FRANCISCO: MARKET & OCTAVIA CASE STUDY

Photo 4.5

SF Park curbside parking payment machine

Yet, as with many of the other transportation components, there has been a severe deficit of political will to adequately expand or manage on-street parking in an equitable way. In 2014, a citywide backlash led to no further expansion of SF Park, despite the success of the program in meeting program goals, and despite plans such as Market and Octavia calling for more robust curbside parking reform. Moreover, as of 2015, there has been little political will to redraw maps of RPP zones or to reform the permit system to make it more functional.

Affordable housing

In addition to reducing car dependency through parking reform, a central goal of the Market and Octavia Plan is to enable households of all incomes and demographics to have an opportunity to live in the transit-oriented core of the city. This is critical because San Francisco has a seemingly insatiable demand for housing, paired with residential construction rates not keeping pace with demand, which has resulted in some of the most expensive housing prices in the world. In San Francisco, even housing without parking can be inaccessible to low- and middle-income households.

In response to emerging concerns over affordability and equity, when the Central Freeway was removed, half of the land that was once underneath the elevated roadway was allotted to lower-income residential development. The politically brokered arrangement required that half of the land be disposed of at market rate, with the sale proceeds underwriting the construction of the new Octavia Boulevard and also for local traffic impact mitigation. The other half of the land had to be used for affordable housing, coordinated by the city but built by nonprofit housing organizations. For example, one of the former freeway parcels must include below-market-rate "family" housing, and as of April 2015 was slated for over 100 units (it should also be noted that waiving parking made affordable housing more feasible). Group housing for formerly homeless and for transitional youth are also part of the mix (and also financially feasible with waived parking requirements). The freeway parcels, when built out, will contain roughly 500 affordable housing units (San Francisco Office of Economic and Workforce Development 2012).

Beyond the freeway parcels, the Market and Octavia Plan also includes a two-tiered affordable housing impact fee. In the busy transit node closest to downtown San Francisco, at the intersection of Market and Van Ness Streets, an $8 per square foot fee is levied on the high-rise towers allowed here. A $4 per square foot fee applies to development in the moderately dense neighborhood commercial transit-oriented zone that spans most of Hayes Valley, the freeway parcels and Market Street (SFPD 2014). This special fee is to be paid into the city's affordable housing fund; however, due to state legal restrictions, it cannot be explicitly dedicated to housing in the immediate area, which, as will be discussed below, is one of the shortcomings of the plan. The zoning code can only "encourage" use of the fee within or nearby the plan area.

The special Market and Octavia affordable housing impact fee is a supplement to the preexisting citywide affordable housing requirement, which requires that any development of over 10 units must provide 12 percent below-market-rate units on-site, or a substantially higher equivalent off-site in the form of fees paid to the city housing fund. Combined, the Market and Octavia fees and the citywide fees, at full buildout, could result in more units of affordable housing than normally required citywide. At present, roughly 16 percent of new housing will be affordable, but add to that the requirements on the freeway parcels, on which half of the parcels must be dedicated to affordable housing, substantially more housing built in the plan will presumably be affordable to lower- and middle-income households.

Urban design

To maintain the existing character and livability of the neighborhoods, while also enabling 6,000 infill units, new design standards were adopted in the plan area.

BUILDING DESIGN

In the neighborhood commercial/transit-oriented zones, active ground floors are required. Regulations on doors and windows, generous ground floor retail ceiling heights, and restrictions on curb cuts and garages were meant to strengthen neighborhood-scaled, walkable streets and to contribute to both a sense of community and safety through "eyes on the street." In the residential transit-oriented areas, small lot sizes are maintained, and small-scale corner stores allowed, but all other commercial activity is limited. In the denser area closer to downtown, building heights ranging from 20- to 40-story towers are allowed, but with strict requirements for narrow towers in order to mitigate high wind speeds at sidewalk level, and to maintain views and decrease skyline clutter. The new residential towers must also

4: SAN FRANCISCO: MARKET & OCTAVIA CASE STUDY

Photo 4.6

Cafe and street life on Market Street

contribute to the creation of signature entryways into this part of the city, and enhance the creation of grand boulevards on Market Street and Van Ness Avenue. Lastly, historic preservation and maximum lot sizes protect much of the Victorian housing stock from demolition, and post-1906 earthquake apartment buildings also have a layer of protection.

LAND USE DESIGN

The Market and Octavia Plan is designed to encourage mixed-use development, and all new housing built in the neighborhood commercial and downtown zoning district must include ground floor retail or commercial activity. Thus far, approximately 90,000 square feet of retail space has been built, with another 74,300 square feet under construction or planed (SFPD 2015). Two modest-sized grocery stores have been approved in the plan area, one built (Whole Foods Dolores) and one under construction (555 Fulton), ensuring that grocery shopping is within adequate walking or bicycling distance to residents.

PUBLIC SPACE DESIGN

The Market and Octavia area is a dense neighborhood but with few parks. It also lacks suitable land for establishing new parks, and so when the freeway was removed, a former freeway parcel was designated as a small park and public gathering space. Known today as "Patricia's Green in Hayes Valley," this park acts as a town square with ample seating, vibrant people watching and space for rotating public art exhibits. To commemorate the political advocacy that led to freeway removal, Patricia Walkup, who spearheaded the campaigns, is recognized as the namesake. Patricia's Green is intensively used, and by itself it falls short of adequate green space for thousands of new housing units, so planners sought other ways to provide public space.

One example of innovative urban design in the Market and Octavia Plan also is the call for transforming alleys, which are now largely used for parking, into pedestrianized green spaces and public plazas. The first "living alleyway" (commonly referred to as woonerf in Europe) is located on Linden Street, between Octavia and Gough, and was made possible through a large amount of citizen interest and involvement. Although resident support for additional living alleyways is high, a common issue is

4: SAN FRANCISCO: MARKET & OCTAVIA CASE STUDY

Photo 4.7

Residential buildings with ground floor retail and restaurants in Market and Octavia area

Source: Photo by Devin Smith

Photo 4.8

Art exhibit and children's playground on Patricia's Green in Market and Octavia area

4: SAN FRANCISCO: MARKET & OCTAVIA CASE STUDY

Photo 4.9

Patricia's Green public plaza space in Market and Octavia area

Photo 4.10

Linden Street living alleyway in Market and Octavia area

> **BOX 4.3 PARKLETS**
>
> Parklets create small but meaningful public spaces for residents within easy walking and biking distances of their homes. Parklets repurpose part of the street next to the sidewalk into a public space for people. These small parks provide amenities such as seating, planting, bicycle parking and art. While they are funded and maintained by neighboring businesses, residents and community organizations, they are publicly accessible and open to all. They also reflect the city's commitment to encouraging equitable walking and bicycling opportunities.
>
> Parklets are a key component of San Francisco's Pavement to Parks program. The Pavement to Parks program is part of San Francisco's larger strategy for creating complete streets and new public open space. Open spaces created through the Pavement to Parks program supplement San Francisco's greater supply of parks and playgrounds. Not all of these amenities are evenly distributed throughout the city, thereby requiring that some residents must travel farther than others for the simple pleasure of enjoying a park or public open space.
>
> The world's first formal public parklets were created in San Francisco in 2010. As of March 2015, over 50 parklets have been installed throughout the city by merchants, neighborhood groups and other organizations. The program has received worldwide acknowledgement and has spread throughout cities across the globe.
>
> The following are Parklet goals as described in the San Francisco Parklet Manual:
>
> > REIMAGINE THE POTENTIAL OF CITY STREETS—Complete streets balance the needs of people walking, riding bicycles, taking transit and travelling by car. Parklets are a relatively low-cost, easily implementable approach to achieving better balance for all users of the street.
> >
> > ENCOURAGE NON-MOTORIZED TRANSPORTATION—Parklets encourage walking by providing pedestrian amenities like public seating, landscaping, and public art. Parklets often provide bicycle parking which makes it easier for people to make the choice to bicycle.
> >
> > ENCOURAGE PEDESTRIAN SAFETY & ACTIVITY—Parklets provide buffer areas between traffic lanes and the sidewalk. They also provide outdoor gathering places in areas where city parks are few or far away.
> >
> > FOSTER NEIGHBORHOOD INTERACTION—Parklets invite pedestrians to sit and gather with friends and neighbors. In many cases, neighbors have participated in the design, financing, construction, and stewardship of parklets.
> >
> > SUPPORT LOCAL BUSINESSES—Parklets enhance the pedestrian environment which can help make the street feel more safe and comfortable for people shopping, running errands, and accessing services in their in their own neighborhoods.
>
> —Andrea Contreras, San Francisco Planning Department

lack of funding and interest from property owners. Many of the alleys are dominated by rental units and tenants cannot provide financial support. As of 2015, several new living alley proposals have surfaced in parts of Hayes Valley, where business owners—particularly restaurants and bars—were very interested in outdoor spaces for patrons.

Another innovative design measure being implemented in the Market and Octavia area, in addition to other areas of the city, are "parklets." Parklets are small-scale green spaces or other publicly

Photo 4.11

Parklet in Market and Octavia area

Source: Photo by Jamie Parks

> **BOX 4.4 PROPOSITION 13**
> Impact fees are important to planning in California because it is very difficult to raise property taxes since the voter-approved "Proposition 13" in 1978, which froze property taxes to 1975 values and then allowed a 2 percent increase annually, with no reassessment of value until property is transferred. When sold, the new rate is only 1 percent of the value of the property. Prop 13 was accompanied by raising the voter thresholds (from 50 percent to 66.6 percent) for new infrastructure taxes, such as transportation or housing, making such taxes less politically feasible. Part of wider antigovernment rebellion dominated by California suburbs (San Francisco voters opposed Prop 13), the outcome significantly reduced local government revenue for transit and other infrastructure. Cities such as San Francisco have become reliant on impact fees instead, which do not require voter approval and are more politically palpable, although not without conflict over the rate of the fees.

accessible open spaces that take the place of curbside parking. Often located in front of businesses, parklets in Hayes Valley, like living alleys, are a strategy to provide green space or public space in an area with a dearth of opportunity sites for parks or plazas.

Community impact fees

To adequately accommodate new housing, the Market and Octavia Plan includes a schedule of impact fees on all new residential and commercial development in the plan area. Impact fees are fees imposed by the city on development projects in order to mitigate the impacts of the new development on public services, infrastructure and facilities. The fee must show a relationship to new development and its impact on existing conditions.

The community improvement fees for Market and Octavia are designed to reflect 20 years of growth and 6,000 new housing units. The types of projects that would be constructed with fee revenue—transit, parks, child-care centers—were determined by residents participating in the planning process, coupled with other citywide goals. The fee rate was established through a political process and can only fund new needs, not needs that existed prior to the plan. As of 2015, the fee rate was $10 per square foot for residential development and $4 per square foot for retail (SFPD 2014). Development impact fees will bring in $60 to $70 million over the life of the plan, but this is short of the $250 million (in 2008 dollars) that was identified in the requisite nexus study for the Market and Octavia Plan's infrastructure needs. To be sure, these funds can be leveraged against local, state and federal "matching funds," especially for transportation investments.

The types of projects that the fees fund include the portion of the new Van Ness bus rapid transit (BRT) line that will traverse the area, transit vehicle capacity that is affected by growth induced by the plan, pedestrian and bicycle enhancements, parks and open space, "living alleys" on lightly trafficked streets and child-care facilities. The impact fees also fund staffing of the community advisory committee and can go toward studying further removal of the Central Freeway and reform of on-street curbside parking.

Community advisory committee

When the Market and Octavia Plan was adopted, a community advisory committee was established. It includes 11 members with four-year terms who are appointed by the Board of Supervisors (equivalent to city council) and Mayor. The committee meets monthly and is charged with prioritizing the order of capital improvements, and additional studies of the plan. It is also charged with developing a five-year monitoring report that identifies what works and what doesn't. The most recent report was published in December 2015. The committee must include renters, low-income residents, business owners and homeowners, and all must either live or work in the plan area.

Public transportation

The Market and Octavia area is well served by transit. More than 10 bus routes and a streetcar, operated by the San Francisco Municipal Transportation Agency (the transit arm of which is commonly referred to as "Muni"), have stops in the area. There are also two underground transit stations in the area that are served by six Muni light rail lines, which alternate between underground service, above-ground segregated service and above-ground service in mixed traffic flow. In addition, two Bay Area Rapid Transit (BART) stations are located within a quarter-mile of the plan area, providing access to commuter rail service across the San Francisco Bay Area region. Due to this excellent transit accessibility, residents of the Market and Octavia area can reach all four corners of the city of San Francisco and more than 600,000 jobs on transit within 40 minutes (SFMTA Interactive Transit Service Map).

The San Francisco Bay Area is served by more than 20 transit agencies. Muni is the transit operator within the City of San Francisco, but several other agencies, such as BART, provide service between San Francisco and other cities within the region. The agencies are fairly well integrated; for example, BART and Muni light rail lines share several underground subway stations. Furthermore, the region has an integrated transit fare payment contactless smartcard called the Clipper Card, which helps to facilitate faster boarding and easier transfers between systems. To further decrease boarding time and increase transit speed and reliability, Muni has recently implemented an all-door boarding policy, which has had positive impacts on system performance.

4: SAN FRANCISCO: MARKET & OCTAVIA CASE STUDY

Photo 4.12

Green bike lane and red transit-only lanes on Market Street

While transit service provision in San Francisco is high, transit demand is also extremely high, and crowding is often an issue. Muni is implementing projects across the city to increase transit capacity, particularly in high-demand areas. The most significant transit improvement related to the Market and Octavia Plan is the proposed Van Ness BRT project, which, when built, will include fully separated bus lanes with all-door boarding and low-floor transit vehicles operating similar to a light rail configuration. The BRT project runs through the eastern side of the plan area. Beyond providing improved transit service, its implementation is expected to help reduce or minimize car traffic through the area. Similarly, a planned east-west BRT project to the north of the plan area, which will run along Geary Boulevard, is expected to help draw away some of the east-west traffic. Both BRT projects, still in the planning phase as of 2015, were proposed in the 1990s as citywide mitigations to the removal of the Central Freeway.

In addition to BRT, several other projects are currently being implemented to help address capacity issues on routes serving the plan area, such as Route 6 and Route 7, which run along Haight Street, carrying upwards of 20,000 passengers daily, and Route 5, which runs along Fulton Street and carries 15,000 passengers daily. These lines are at capacity. In response, Muni is incrementally upgrading the routes with exclusive "red carpet" transit lanes on Haight Street and Market Street, and new bus stop and transit signal priority on both the Haight and Fulton routes. The lateral (north-south) Route 22-Fillmore bus line also has a short segment of red carpet transit lanes to the south of the plan area on Church Street.

Bicycle and pedestrian infrastructure

Many people in the Market and Octavia area are inclined to walk or bike. The distances are reasonable, there are ways to circumvent steep inclines, and transit alternatives in the area are often crowded. Bicycling has increased dramatically throughout the city, and much of this new bicycle traffic traverses the Market and Octavia Plan area. As mentioned, the "Wiggle," which passes through the area, is a bicycle route of citywide importance because it enables one to bike across the city without having to encounter many steep grades.

4: SAN FRANCISCO: MARKET & OCTAVIA CASE STUDY

Photo 4.13

Contraflow red bus-only lane on Haight Street

Photo 4.14

Red bus-only lanes, green bike lane and soft-hit posts on Market Street

4: SAN FRANCISCO: MARKET & OCTAVIA CASE STUDY

Photo 4.15 *(top left)*

Green bike lane and bicycle counter on Market Street

Photo 4.16 *(top right)*

Cycle track and bicycle signal head on Market Street

Photo 4.17 *(left)*

Bike-share station and green bike lane on Market Street

Effective bicycle infrastructure has been implemented in the Market and Octavia Plan area, including green bike lanes and innovative soft-hit posts. Green bike lanes have been painted on Market Street between Van Ness and 10th Street, and an innovative use of soft-hit posts has been deployed. This cheap but meaningful infrastructure could be expanded throughout the entire Market and Octavia Plan area in a very short amount of time. Bicycle-specific traffic signal heads have also been implemented on Market Street to help direct bicycle travel. Bicycles are given their own phase at traffic lights to protect them from turning vehicles.

Pedestrian improvements implemented in the area include intersection treatments with new crosswalks and pedestrian bulb-outs. Many of the pedestrian improvements are dovetailed with transit enhancements.

Carsharing

Carsharing was in its infancy when the plan was originally crafted, but since adoption carshare has been required as part of the parking in new developments. City Carshare, a nonprofit carsharing organization that has been operating in the San Francisco Bay area since 2001, has approximately 30 carsharing vehicles located within the plan area (https://citycarshare.org/). Zipcar, a for-profit carsharing organization operating nationwide, has 35 carsharing vehicles located within the plan area (www.zipcar.com/). The SFTMA is testing a pilot project to create curbside carshare on selected streets in the plan area, as well as other parts of the city. In July 2015, the first curbside carshare pods were installed in the plan area, and more pods will be established.

Bike sharing

Bay Area Bike Share has 700 bikes and 70 stations located in the cities of San Francisco, Redwood City, Mountain View, Palo Alto and San Jose. Stations were specifically located near Caltrain, commuter rail stations with the intention of providing a first-mile or last-mile connection to Caltrain. The system will be expanded tenfold, to include 7,000 bikes in 2016 and 2017, adding cities east of San Francisco to the system, including Berkeley, Emeryville and Oakland. Of the additional bikes, more than half are expected to be located in San Francisco. Currently, only two bike-share stations are located in the Market and Octavia area, but the first phase of expansion includes the Hayes Valley and Upper Market neighborhoods, so much of the plan area will see bike share in late 2016 or early 2017 (www.bayareabikeshare.com/).

QUANTITATIVE ANALYSIS

The Market and Octavia area is located in one of the most politically progressive cities in the United States when it comes to transportation policies. These policies have helped to make Market and Octavia what it is today. However, not all neighborhoods in the city have benefited from the recent urban infill development opportunities paired with a masterplanning process geared toward sustainable transportation, as was the case with Market and Octavia. For example, the Marina district, also located less than two miles from the downtown city center, has much more car-centric design and policy measures, including lower levels of transit access, only a handful of carsharing vehicles, fewer goods and services within walking

Table 4.1 Statistics for Market and Octavia, the Marina, and City of San Francisco

	Market and Octavia	The Marina	City of San Francisco
Population	30,800	22,800	850,000
Area (acres)	740	640	30,000
Population density (persons/acre)	42	36	28
Cars per 1,000 residents	400	650	470
Percentage of households with zero cars	44%	20%	30%
Mode share for commute trips			
Car	35%	50%	48%
Public transit	40%	31%	33%
Bike	7%	2%	3%
Walk	9%	4%	10%
Telecommute	8%	11%	7%

Sources: ACS (2006–2010), Census Journey to Work Data (2008–2012), SFPD (2015)

access and less restrictive parking policies. Various metrics are compared between the Market and Octavia area, the Marina district and the City of San Francisco to demonstrate the reductions in car dependency enjoyed by Market and Octavia area residents (see Table 4.1).

Car ownership rates

As Figure 4.2 shows, based on data collected through the American Community Survey, the car ownership rate for the City of San Francisco is 470 vehicles per 1,000 residents, which is much lower than for other cities in the United States, which typically range from 600 to 900 vehicles per 1,000 residents. Car ownership in the Market and Octavia area is even lower than the average for the city of San Francisco at 400 vehicles per 1,000 residents. By contrast, car ownership rates in the Marina district are much higher, at 650 vehicles per 1,000 residents. This demonstrates that the design measures and policies in place in the Market and Octavia area have been successful at maintaining low car ownership rates among residents, which has a strong influence on keeping vehicle miles traveled (VMT) and GHG emissions low.

Automobile density

Parking is one of the keystones of the Market and Octavia Plan. Limiting residential off-street parking is the corollary to maintaining low car ownership rates. While the city has not tracked the cumulative amount of new off-street parking produced in the plan area, preliminary data suggest that almost all new housing developments are building parking at rates conforming with the plan, and several projects have been approved with zero residential parking. The cumulative off-street parking ratio is approximately 0.5–0.6:1 (Millard-Ball 2015).

The Market and Octavia Plan's parking policies are an acknowledgment that too many cars ruin density. Enabling increased population density and increasing the intensity and mix of uses must not be accompanied by significant increases in automobile density, or the compact geography of the plan area will be oversaturated with cars. Figure 4.3 shows the cars per square mile, based on car ownership rates determined through American Community Survey data, in San Francisco, the Market and Octavia area and the Marina. The Market and Octavia area does have a higher density of cars than the City of San Francisco, primarily because, although the car ownership rate per person is higher for the city, the population density is higher in the Market and Octavia area. The density of automobiles in the Marina is much higher, at more than 14,000 cars per square mile. This high concentration of cars in a small amount of spaces leads to increased traffic and escalated parking issues.

4: SAN FRANCISCO: MARKET & OCTAVIA CASE STUDY

Figure 4.2

Car ownership rates in San Francisco, Market and Octavia, and the Marina

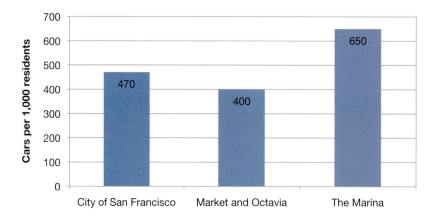

Figure 4.3

Car density in San Francisco, Market and Octavia, and the Marina

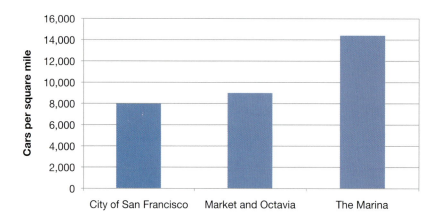

Commute mode share

With reduced parking and car ownership rates hovering at around 400 cars per 1,000 residents, walking, biking and transit mode shares should be high in Market and Octavia. The close proximity to downtown San Francisco and to so many nearby vibrant and walkable neighborhoods also lends to less driving and more walking, biking, and transit use.

Figure 4.4 shows that, according to Census Journey to Work survey data, while auto commute mode share remains fairly constant at around 50 percent between 1990 and 2012 for the City of San Francisco, auto commute mode share for the Market and Octavia area is decreasing over time, particularly as new developments with stricter parking policies are being built. The auto commute mode share for the area decreases from 48 percent in 1990 to 35 percent in the 2008–2012 Census Journey to Work 5-Year Estimates. During the same period, bike commute mode share increased from 1 percent to 7 percent. Meanwhile, auto commute mode share for the Marina district is higher, varying from 50 percent to 57 percent, and is lowest during the 2008–2012 time period at 50 percent. During the 2008–2012 time period, the telecommute mode share jumps for all areas, indicating changes in the economy and more flexible work schedules. The Marina district in particular has a high telecommute mode share in 2008–2012 of 11 percent.

It should be noted that commutes in San Francisco are continuing to evolve. Since the Market and Octavia Plan was adopted, there has been a proliferation of privatized corporate commuter buses for large technology companies located in Silicon Valley but with a high portion of their workforce living in San Francisco. Packs of these buses are visible every weekday morning and evening on Church Street near Market Street, on Van Ness Avenue, and on Hayes Street. Initial studies by city agencies have found that while these private shuttles reduce private car use, they also reduce commute-purpose transit

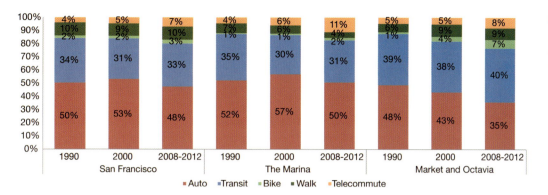

Figure 4.4

Commute mode shares for San Francisco, the Marina, and Market and Octavia

Source: Analysis by Kristen Carnarius

trips. In 2014, the SFMTA initiated a monitoring study of this ad hoc privatized system. Without better data collection, it is difficult to assess the mode share for these private buses, but anecdotally they have a big presence.

Vehicle miles traveled

In California, as mentioned in the introduction, VMT is a proxy for carbon emissions from automobiles. Though not exact, California's climate change and land use policy, Senate Bill 375, mandates that regional planners show reductions in VMT. Partly in response, the City of San Francisco has developed new ways for estimating VMT and linking it to land use.

The City of San Francisco has a state-of-the-art travel demand model that is used to evaluate proposed transportation and land use projects in the city. The travel model, known as SF-CHAMP (San Francisco Chained Activity Modeling Process) is used to assess the impacts of land use, socioeconomic and transportation system changes on the performance of the local transportation system. SF-CHAMP was developed to reflect San Francisco's unique transportation system and socioeconomic and land use characteristics. It uses San Francisco residents' observed travel patterns, detailed representations of San Francisco's transportation system, population and employment characteristics, transit line boardings, roadway volumes, and the number of vehicles available to San Francisco households to produce measures relevant to transportation and land use planning. Using future year transportation, land use and socioeconomic inputs, the model forecasts future travel demand (www.sfcta.org/modeling-and-travel-forecasting).

SF-CHAMP produces records of simulated trips for the population of the San Francisco Bay Area over the course of a day, and that data can be used to derive trip mode share and average vehicle miles traveled (VMT) per resident and household. Figure 4.5 shows a map of average daily VMT per household across the City of San Francisco. The Market and Octavia area, the Marina district and Downtown San Francisco are outlined. Areas in Downtown San Francisco have the lowest average daily VMT rates of any area in the city, and VMT per household increases progressively the further the household distance from downtown.

These VMT estimates are the result of a travel demand model and not the results of surveys or observations of residents, workers or visitors, although travel survey data, observed traffic volumes and transit ridership and other data were used to estimate, calibrate and validate the model. When estimating travel decisions of Bay Area residents, the model takes into consideration many of the factors highlighted in this case study, including density and mix of uses, transit service provision and connectivity, and proximity to downtown. Higher densities and mixes of uses enable more people to walk or bike to destinations rather than driving. Higher levels of transit service enable more people to take transit as an alternative to driving. Proximity to downtown and the high concentration of jobs located there provides more opportunities for residents to walk or bike to work, further contributing to reductions in VMT.

Figure 4.6 shows the average daily VMT per resident and per household for the Market and Octavia area, the Marina district, and the City of San Francisco. Despite the fact that the two areas are located

4: SAN FRANCISCO: MARKET & OCTAVIA CASE STUDY

Figure 4.5

Map of San Francisco VMT per household

Source: Map by Drew Cooper

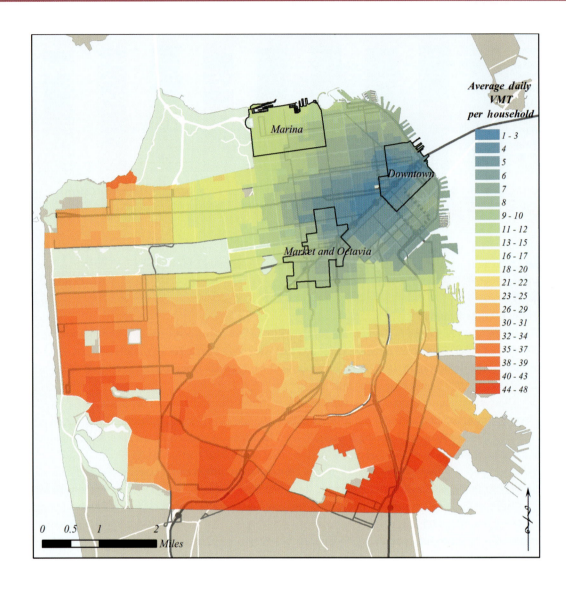

a similar distance from downtown, the Marina district has higher VMT values than Market and Octavia, due, in part, to the Market and Octavia area having higher densities, higher provision of transit and a higher proportion of car-free households. The topography also comes into play as there is a hill located between the Marina and Downtown. However, both areas have much lower VMT than in other parts of the city, which are located further from downtown and have lower densities and less transit provision.

This suggests that locating new development within an area such as Market and Octavia would result in lower average VMT for residents and employees than if that development were located in another part of the city with lower densities, mix of uses and transit provision.

While the SF-CHAMP model includes some information about parking pricing, it does not consider other inputs related to parking policies being implemented in the Market and Octavia area such as unbundled parking and reduced parking provision rates in new developments. It also does not consider specific design measures such as provision of public space or pedestrian infrastructure. These policy and design measures could lead to even lower levels of VMT generated than those estimated by the model.

LESSONS LEARNED

The Market and Octavia Plan offers important lessons for low carbon planning. Reducing GHGs is a formal goal of California, and Senate Bill 375 requires regional land use and transportation plans reduce

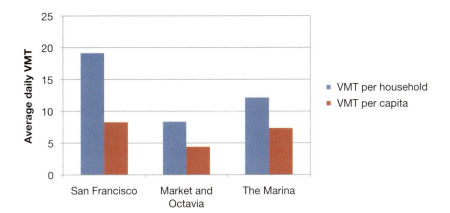

Figure 4.6

Average daily VMT for San Francisco, Market and Octavia, and the Marina

carbon emissions from transportation. As of 2015, California is the only state in the United States that mandates linking emissions reduction to regional planning. "Plan Bay Area," which is a regional transportation and land use plan for the nine-county metropolitan area, includes accommodating two million new residents all within the existing built-up footprint of the Bay Area, and with most of the growth steered toward priority development areas (PDAs) situated around regional transit nodes. Market and Octavia is one of these PDAs.

In the City of San Francisco, planners expect that 92,000 housing units and 190,000 new jobs will be added to San Francisco by 2040, increasing the city's current population from 850,000 to over one million (ABAG and MTC 2013). Getting the Market and Octavia Plan right is critical to maintain momentum toward residential and commercial infill and providing a model for the rest of the Bay Area, as well as American urban planning in general. Learning what has not gone right is also critical, so that next generation planning can make amends and produce both more livable and equitable cities.

Compared to previous planning regimes in San Francisco, the Market and Octavia Plan is a success story, but there are some critical lessons to be gleaned from the plan's implementation that would constructively aid in better planning throughout San Francisco and the Bay Area, as well as low carbon communities worldwide.

Urban freeway removal

The Market and Octavia Plan area is an example of the benefits associated with urban freeway removal. First and foremost, removing the freeway north of Market Street provided over seven acres of new land for housing in a city that was built out by the early 1950s. More broadly, the lessons of the freeway removal come at an opportune moment. Much of North America's aging urban freeway system is approaching 50, 60 and even 70 years of service. The American Society of Civil Engineers (2009) warns that one-third of the nation's major roads and freeways are unsound and that 26 percent of bridges are structurally deficient. The nation's urban freeway infrastructure, especially bridges and elevated freeways, must be overhauled, and this will bring disruptions to traffic flows while also being very costly. Given this gloomy picture, some people are asking, why not just tear down some of the old freeways and rethink urban transportation (Congress for the New Urbanism 2012)?

Housing

The most obvious success of Market and Octavia is that it is accommodating a fair amount of new housing. As of 2015, almost all of the opportunity sites for housing, including the seven acres of the former freeway parcels, had been either built out or were in the development pipeline. On paper, there is no longer any vacant land in the plan area, and barring any significant economic recession (such as the 2009 financial crisis), the plan will likely build out in the early 2020s. By legalizing in-law units (an additional separate living space located on a property where only one unit would normally be) and decoupling off-street parking from housing, more housing may be potentially affordable for a diverse array of incomes and lifestyles. By preserving the preexisting housing stock, the plan also preserves existing rent-controlled units, which staves off some of the impact of gentrification but also puts upward pressure on market rate.

Despite these efforts, affordability is a major problem in San Francisco, and not something that can be attributed to the plan itself. However, the plan has made the neighborhoods within the plan area extremely desirable, adding a premium to the already high housing prices. The affordable housing impact fees and the city inclusionary laws are helpful, but not the panacea.

The goal of inclusionary housing is critical for low carbon development. Without it, households unable to afford San Francisco will be displaced to far-flung suburbs, and will either be enslaved to long transit commutes to city jobs, or opt to purchase a first or second car. Including housing for all incomes was therefore a priority for the Hayes Valley Neighborhood Association and other neighborhood groups in the Market and Octavia planning process.

However, developers are allowed to forego on-site affordable housing if they pay an equivalent and slightly higher fee to the city. Many of the developers have opted to do this, and thus less affordable housing has been built than what was possible (the housing is required to be built within the city, but not the plan area). Since land is costly in the plan area, the city does not intend to build much affordable housing itself, except on the designated freeway parcels. Out of 900 units, about 45 percent would be constructed as affordable housing on the former freeway parcels, but the pace of construction has lagged behind market-rate housing. In the rest of the plan area, over 800 units have been or will be built under the city's inclusionary housing requirement, approximately 16 percent of new housing in the pipeline. Some developers have opted to "fee-out," and where that housing was built is anyone's guess, but it has not come to Market and Octavia.

Further, the affordable housing that is built in the plan area is dedicated to the lowest income brackets, such as low-income seniors, the disabled or transitional youth and formerly homeless populations. Middle-class housing is not being produced, and only affluent newcomers can afford the extremely high rents ($3,500 per month for a one bedroom), and with new for-sale units fetching more than $1,000 per square foot, the middle class is excluded from choosing to live in Market and Octavia.

It is clear that city laws need to be revised to require that all affordable housing be built on-site or at least within the plan area, and moreover it may be time for the city to increase the requirement from 12 percent to 20 percent or higher. Some neighborhood groups are insisting on 20 percent in return for their political support, and in adjacent South of Market neighborhood, the supervisor representing the area is promoting 30 percent affordability for new development.

As of 2015, there was a vigorous and increasingly urgent discussion about affordable housing among San Francisco's political establishment. A key part of that discussion is how to produce middle-class housing—housing for teachers, public safety officers and even city planners. Because the market is providing only high-end housing, ideas of using public lands (such as freeway parcels or excess city property) are on the table but there is scarce land. Long-term, viable solutions that meet the scale of the problem are lacking.

Regardless of whether other cities hoping to build new low carbon developments have the same affordability issues as San Francisco or not, accommodating a mix of income levels should be a goal. Various mechanisms can be put in place to facilitate this goal, such as requirements that a certain portion of new housing be low-income. Providing a mix of unit sizes and tenure types can also help to ensure that the housing stock can accommodate a range of potential residents.

Parking

All things considered, when compared to the previous paradigm of development, the plan's parking policies are working. The ratio of parking for new housing is estimated at between 0.5 and 0.6 parking spaces per residential unit (Millard-Ball 2015). With the exception of one intransigent developer in the earliest phase of the plan, almost all subsequent development has stayed within the plan's parking parameters, although not without low-level political struggle. There have been a small handful of car-free projects as well. The San Francisco Jazz performing arts venue (and offices) was built without parking, and a development that includes 69 units of housing and a youth recreation center is also car-free. Affordable housing projects on the Octavia Boulevard and on Market Street have come in with zero parking, and it is clear that relaxing parking has made nonprofit social services and housing more viable. In April 2015, a market-rate development off of Market Street, and one block from future Van Ness BRT, was proposed. However, disappointingly, few residential developments between 2009 and 2015 proposed "zero" parking. It should also be noted that new development is required to have bicycle parking for residents, as part of new citywide regulations, and that all developments in Market and Octavia have followed that requirement.

Data on car ownership rates corroborate the positive outcome with respect to parking. Car ownership in the plan area has stayed modest, at 400 cars per 1,000 residents.

One reason why the innovative off-street parking policies of the Market and Octavia Plan have worked so well is because the Planning Department both crafted the policy and is responsible for the zoning. Other cities can learn from this example by updating zoning codes to include parking maximums, capping parking in ways that discourage car ownership. This should replace obsolete zoning codes still in place in many cities, which require a minimum amount of parking to be built per land use type. This type of policy leads to cities being over-parked, providing more parking spaces than are needed and reducing the walkability and livability of neighborhoods. In order to create low carbon communities, the number of parking spaces provided in neighborhoods should be limited.

Traffic calming

Transportation impacts have been slow to realize and make up a key shortcoming of the plan. When the freeway was removed and before the Octavia Boulevard was completed (2003–2005), the streets of Hayes Valley were quiet, calm and decidedly livable. Page Street was a pleasant street to bicycle, and the Haight Street buses ran reliably and with ease.

Yet, when the Boulevard and rebuilt freeway opened in 2005, automobile traffic quickly overwhelmed the Hayes Valley portion of the plan area. Morning and afternoon peak traffic spills from inbound Oak Street over to Page and Haight Streets, impeding buses and bicyclists. This has also created dangerous conditions at many intersections and can be discouraging to bicycling.

However, the plan did call for the reintroduction of two-way streets on some previously one-way streets, and these have been slowly implemented. On Hayes Street, a two-block segment between Gough and Van Ness was reverted to two-way, and this has substantially calmed the traffic patterns and improved walkability. Additionally, several crosswalks were re-established after having been removed during the freeway era. On Haight Street, a contraflow bus lane was established on what was previously a one-way segment feeding traffic to the Octavia Boulevard and freeway. Previously, the buses on Haight Street were persistently delayed by queuing traffic. The buses also had to make an awkward and time-consuming block-long jog as part of a traffic scheme imposed to make Haight Street one-way for one block, feeding cars to the Boulevard. The elimination of the jog, addition of the contraflow bus lane and extension of the bus lane two blocks westward on Haight has substantially reduced transit travel times through the neighborhood.

A substantial percentage of the traffic that saturates the Market and Octavia area is citywide and regional in origin. Looking long-term, a citywide approach of "metering" traffic upstream, such as Oak and Fell to the west, and Franklin and Gough to the north and south, as well as metering egress from freeways to city streets, could be implemented. Congestion pricing, proposed but yet to be taken seriously in the political establishment, could also help reduce traffic in the neighborhood area.

Other cities considering urban freeway removal should pay close attention to the potential routing of vehicles onto city streets resulting from the removal of a freeway segment, and should implement traffic-calming measures to ensure that traffic coming off of the freeway is sufficiently slowed and dispersed in order to reduce negative traffic impacts to the surrounding neighborhoods.

Urban design

Urban design guidelines have been far-reaching and successful. With a few exceptions, the plan's guidelines have encouraged more innovative modern architecture and design than what was previously allowed, and has successfully minimized the impact of garage doors and curbs cuts at the pedestrian interface. At the sidewalk level, requiring active uses in new infill projects has improved walkability; however, due to the rapid rise in commercial rents, there remain vacant storefronts in some buildings on Market Street and nearby.

Two innovative urban design measures that have been implemented in the Market and Octavia area, opening up additional space for public use, are the "living alleyway" and the parklet. Both of these concepts have had positive impacts on the Market and Octavia area, and can be implemented in other cities in order to create vibrant public spaces in constrained urban areas.

Interagency coordination

San Francisco has multiple city agencies governing housing and transit. In the early years of the Market and Octavia Plan, there was a critical disconnect between the SFMTA and the City Planning Department. The SFMTA was in the throes of fiscal crisis, service was cut, and funds for traffic calming and other programs in short supply. Additionally, with development stalled, impact fee revenue was not coming in.

However, in 2011, a new director came to the SFMTA, and the agency began to focus more on livability. Interagency coordination quickly improved, and the SFMTA's livable streets goals aligned very closely with the Market and Octavia Plan goals. Today, the SFMTA is closely involved with the Community Advisory Committee and coordinates frequently with the Planning Department. Transit has especially started to improve relative to the early phase of the plan, and a new traffic-calming effort, underway in 2014 and 2015, is being enthusiastically pursued by the SFMTA. That said, the reform of curbside parking has lagged. While interagency cooperation is now the norm, for Market and Octavia it was not always so. For other cities, coordination between fragmented city departments should be prioritized when the planning process begins.

Community advisory committee

The community advisory committee has been pivotal in ensuring that the impact fees generated by new development in the plan area are used for projects that meet the goals of the Market and Octavia Plan and serve the neighborhood residents. As with the coordination of local government agencies, including citizens creates a sense of stewardship and empowers residents to shape their community. Participatory planning helps minimize conflict, and it also provides significant institutional memory from longtime residents. This model could be replicated in neighborhoods in other cities to help guide investments made by the city.

Mix of uses

One of the core ideas of a "complete" neighborhood such as Market and Octavia is to encourage small businesses that serve neighborhood needs, particularly for daily needs. Yet, portions of the plan area have not seen local, utilitarian shops open. For example, Hayes Valley has had little new neighborhood-serving activity, but an increase in boutique, destination shopping. In early 2010, one of the last remaining neighborhood-serving businesses, a video store, shut down due, in part, to increased rent. Between 2005 and 2015, it appears that Hayes Valley has experienced deepening retail gentrification such that few actual neighborhood-serving businesses are located in Hayes Valley. Some businesses, such as some restaurants, cater to both local and regional markets, but others are very much regional in scope. The pricing out of utilitarian, neighborhood-serving retail has been an issue in the Market and Octavia Plan area.

One possibility to remedy the retail issue is to provide subsidized rents on the city-owned freeway parcels, perhaps inducing a more affordable local grocer at Hayes and Octavia, for example.

Similarly, other new development should try to encourage neighborhood-serving uses in the area, facilitating the ability of residents to walk or bike to conduct daily needs.

Public transportation

Several measures are being implemented in the Market Octavia Plan area to improve bus speeds and reliability, including red transit-only lanes, transit bus stop bulb-outs and transit signal priority. There are also plans for a BRT project on Van Ness Avenue, which would include exclusive transit lanes on the eastern side of the plan area. However, while the measures implemented address speed and reliability issues, they do not address crowding. As with housing affordability and traffic, transit finance is a conundrum that reaches beyond the Market and Octavia Plan area.

As the Market and Octavia Plan was adopted, between 2005 and 2010, the city actually raised fares and cut service. This has had a very noticeable impact on the Market and Octavia area. On a daily basis, including Saturdays and Sundays, the buses are jam-packed. In the morning, commute-hour buses and trains coming from the west side of San Francisco are at capacity by the time they reach the Hayes Valley neighborhood. There is no spare capacity for future development unless vehicles are added and frequency is increased.

In sum, the influx of new housing and commercial activity in the Market and Octavia area has not been synchronized with much-needed transit capacity expansion and improvement, and the result is the plan area, and especially Hayes Valley, remain saturated with cars passing through the area, with origins and destinations outside the Market and Octavia area.

The lesson learned for other new developments is to ensure that sufficient transit capacity is in place to meet the needs of neighborhood residents, as well as pass-through trips.

Bicycling infrastructure

Many of the streets in the area are very suitable for bicycling and, with the exception of some minor improvements, need little change. Reflecting the dramatic increase in bicycling, and the transit capacity issues, bicycling has great potential if infrastructure is provided. In parts of the area, the bicycle share for all daily trips is probably close to 10 percent and could be substantially higher if cheap, quick infrastructure is deployed rapidly but carefully. Effective bicycle infrastructure that has been implemented in some parts of the Market and Octavia Plan area, including green bike lanes and innovative soft-hit posts, could be expanded to other areas of the neighborhood.

However, every bicyclist is, at some point, affronted with a confusing myriad of heavy-volume, arterial streets splicing through the area. Bicycle safety in the area could be improved through implementation of filtered permeability principles. This would include implementing traffic calming features aimed at making certain routes more direct for bicycles than for cars. The benefits would include reduced traffic speeds and volumes leading to safer bicycling conditions, and faster, more direct routes for bicyclists.

CONCLUSION

Market and Octavia, along with GWL Terrein and Vauban, are examples of development processes initiated by community impetus that explicitly sought to discourage driving and car ownership. In some sense, they are car-free more than car-lite, although with Market and Octavia only roughly half of new units are truly car-free.

While GWL Terrein and Vauban are representative of brownfield sites, with Market and Octavia, while having some land parcels that might qualify as brownfield (such as former gas stations and automobile dealers), the crux of the plan was about infill after removing a freeway. Therefore, the Market and Octavia Plan can serve to inspire many other North American cities considering freeway removal, especially as the politics of possibilities for removing freeways is gaining traction. Milwaukee replaced a freeway stub with a boulevard. In New Orleans, there is a movement to remove an aging elevated freeway that blighted a once-thriving African-American neighborhood. In Seattle, there was a debate about removing the crumbling Alaska Way Viaduct on the city's waterfront. Similarly, the Gardiner Expressway in Toronto has received attention for potential removal. In Washington, DC, in the Bronx, New York, and Syracuse, Louisville, and Providence, removing, tunneling or realigning of freeways has been proposed. San Francisco's experience of removing the Central Freeway can provide many lessons.

NOTES

1. For more details on the planning process, and especially on traffic engineering metrics and parking ratios, see Chapters 3, 4 and 5 in Henderson (2013).
2. Estimate calculated by Adam Millard-Ball (2015), professor of Environmental Studies at UC Santa Cruz, and parking policy expert studying the Market and Octavia Plan.

REFERENCES

American Community Survey (ACS) (2006–2010) *5-Year Estimates, 2006–2010*, available at: www.census.gov/programs-surveys/acs/ (accessed July 2015).

American Society of Civil Engineers (2009) *Report Card for America's Infrastructure*, available at: www.infrastructurereportcard.org/report-cards (accessed July 30, 2012).

Association of Bay Area Governments (ABAG) and Metropolitan Transportation Commission (MTC) (2013) *Plan Bay Area: Regional Transportation Plan and Sustainable Communities Strategy for the San Francisco Bay Area 2013–2040*, Oakland: ABAG/MTC: 154.

City of San Francisco Planning Department (2008) *Market & Octavia: An Area Plan of the General Plan of the City and County of San Francisco*, available at: www.sf-planning.org/ftp/files/Citywide/Market_Octavia/Market_and_Octavia_Area_Plan_2010.pdf (accessed July 2015).

Congress for the New Urbanism (2012) *Freeways without Futures*, Chicago, IL: Congress for the New Urbanism.

Henderson, J. (2013) *Street Fight: The Politics of Mobility in San Francisco*, Amherst, MA: University of Massachusetts Press.

Millard-Ball, A. (2015) "Unpublished manuscript: the causal impacts of urban plans: the case of transit-oriented development. Paper under development," forthcoming.

SFMTA Interactive Transit Service Map: www.ocf.berkeley.edu/~djhoward/transitmap/transit.html.

SFMTA 2013 bicycle strategic plan.

San Francisco Office of Economic and Workforce Development (2012) Octavia Boulevard/Central Freeway Project Update: Presentation to San Francisco Board of Supervisors, Land Use Committee October 29, 2012, San Francisco San Francisco Board of Supervisors, Land Use Committee.

San Francisco Planning Department (SFPD) (2014) *San Francisco Planning Code, Schedule of Impact Fees*, San Francisco, CA: San Francisco Planning Department, available at: http://planning.sanfranciscocode.org/4/416/416.413/.

San Francisco Planning Department (SFPD) (2015) "Unpublished report: San Francisco Planning Department quarterly pipeline reports for Market and Octavia, Q4, 2014," San Francisco, CA: San Francisco Planning Department.

United States Census 2000: www.census.gov/main/www/cen2000.html.

5

Stockholm

Hammarby Sjöstad case study

> **BOX 5.1**
> **HAMMARBY SJÖSTAD SITE FACTS**
>
> *Developer:*
> Multiple[1]
>
> *Architect:*
> Jan Inghe-Hagström[2]
>
> *Population:*
> 20,000
>
> *Projected population:*
> 28,000
>
> *Total area:*
> 400 acres
>
> *Current density:*
> 50 persons/acre
>
> *Projected density:*
> 70 persons/acre
>
> *Current residential units:*
> 10,000
>
> *Projected residential units:*
> 13,000
>
> *Construction began:*
> 1999
>
> *Planned completion:*
> 2017
>
> *Distance from city center:*
> 2 miles
>
> *Cars:*
> 210 cars/1,000 residents
>
> *Parking spaces/residence:*
> 0.65
>
> *Non-motorized mode share:*
> 27%
>
> *Public transport mode share:*
> 52%
>
> *Households with carsharing membership:*
> 18%
>
> 1 Over 30 developers; key developers are JM, Skanska, Family Housing, Swedish Housing, HSB, SKB and Borätt
> 2 Jan Inghe-Hagström designed the strategic masterplan. Other architecture firms involved include: White Architects, Nyréns Architect Firm, and Erséus.

BACKGROUND

Our last three case studies exemplified high levels of participatory planning process. Although not necessarily top-down, the next three case studies exhibit local planning expressions of larger city or even national agendas. The goals of these developments are more explicit expressions of a national focus on promoting sustainability.

Hammarby Sjöstad is Stockholm's signature car-lite development. Stockholm was a city that, in the 1950s and 1960s, was retrofitted for the car (as discussed by Peter Hall (1998) in *Cities and Civilization*). Conscious changes were made to make the city fit the car, effectively dismantling the walkability and human scale of the center of Stockholm. However, the momentum in Stockholm today is toward reversing this legacy of accommodating the car at the expense of livability and stitching the city back together in a car-lite manner. Hammarby Sjöstad is an important step in this direction of putting Stockholm on the path toward sustainable transportation.

Hammarby Sjöstad is a brownfield redevelopment with mixed uses, carsharing, bike sharing, good transit access and high-quality bicycle infrastructure. Car use and transport-related emissions are lower in the development than in comparable reference districts or the city as a whole.

Hammarby Sjöstad is recognized around the globe for having implemented an integrated approach to district planning incorporating sustainable resource use, ecological design and low carbon transport. The 400-acre district was built on a former industrial and harbor brownfield area located on the south side of Hammarby Lake, two miles south of the Stockholm city center. The initiative for redevelopment began in the early 1990s with the Stockholm application for the 2004 Olympic Games and the ambition of creating an ecological Olympic Village. Although Stockholm did not win the bid, planning moved forward and construction of the project began in 1999, converting the site from a run-down industrial area into a modern, environmentally sustainable, mixed-use district with good public transit connections. Nearly 10,000 residential units have been completed and are home to some 20,000 residents. Ultimately, the district will boast 13,000 residential units with a projected 28,000 inhabitants (http://bygg.stockholm.se/hammarbysjostad; Björn Cederquist, pers. comm.).

One key to the success of Hammarby Sjöstad is that from the beginning, planning work was integrated with environmental goals incorporating land use, transportation, building materials, energy, water and sewage, and waste components. All of the authorities and administrations normally involved in the development process collaborated to develop a plan and conceptual approach to the project with a focus on sustainable resource usage. The implementation of a holistic environmental profile for a whole district was a new concept when plans began in 1996.

The city imposed strict environmental requirements on buildings, technical installations and the traffic environment. The goal was to halve the environmental impact compared to a typical development built in the 1990s. The environmental goals set for transportation in Hammarby Sjöstad were (Fränne 2007):

- 80 percent of residents' and workers' journeys made by public transport, bike or foot by 2010;
- at least 15 percent of households having carsharing memberships by 2010;

Photo 5.1

Pedestrian pathways in Hammarby Sjöstad

Source: Photo by Luc Nadal

- at least 5 percent of workplaces having carsharing memberships by 2010; and
- 100 percent of heavy transportation by vehicles meeting environmental zone requirements.

Although no official evaluation of these goals has been conducted, a survey of residents in 2008 found that 79 percent of daily trips made by residents were by public transit, bike or foot, and an Internet-based survey of Hammarby Sjöstad residents conducted in 2010 found that 95 percent of work trips made by residents were by public transit, bike or foot (Brick 2008; ITDP 2010). The 2010 survey also found that 18 percent of households have a carsharing membership. Therefore, although these metrics are not officially being measured, it appears that most of the initial transportation-related environmental goals set for the development are being met.

PLANNING PROCESS

The planning process of Hammarby Sjöstad is notable for the high degree of local authority leadership in every stage from development of the masterplan to construction. The implementation and control of design is facilitated by the fact that the city has acquired most of the land in Hammarby Sjöstad. Furthermore, a politically driven sustainability program is a key part of Hammarby Sjöstad. The program includes targets for decontamination, use of brownfield land, provision of public transit options in order to discourage car use, energy consumption, water conservation and recycling. In addition, since all planning applications in Stockholm are based on life cycle cost analysis, it was easier for the development to justify higher initial investments in better performing building design and transportation infrastructure.

The first step in the planning process was the development of the strategic masterplan, led by architect Jan Inghe-Hagström, at the Stockholm City Planning Bureau. The plan is divided into 12 sub-neighborhoods, which are being developed in phases. A process called "parallel sketches" is being used in which the city selects three to four architects/planners in the private sector to draw up detailed proposals for a sub-neighborhood. The city evaluates each of the sketches and combines the best features to create the agreed upon masterplan.

5: STOCKHOLM: HAMMARBY SJÖSTAD CASE STUDY

Photo 5.2

Hammarby Sjöstad before redevelopment

Source: Photo by Leif Straat

Photo 5.3

Hammarby Sjöstad today

Source: Photo by Lennart Johansson

5: STOCKHOLM: HAMMARBY SJÖSTAD CASE STUDY

Figure 5.1

Map of Hammarby Sjöstad

Source: Map by Amy Smith

The city planning and design team then prepares a design code for each sub-neighborhood in partnership with the developers and architects. This design code is included in the development agreement between the developer and the city. The design code is taken through the local authority political process in order to grant planning permission; the code provides an overview of the layout, form and structure of each block including key landmark buildings, public spaces and pedestrian routes.

In order to provide architectural diversity, and to inspire higher standards of design through competition, a consortium of developers and architects are then invited by the city to develop each plot or individual building within the sub-neighborhood, according to the design code. So far, over 30 different developers and more than 30 architects have been identified. Key developers are JM, Skanska, Family Housing, Swedish Housing, HSB, SKB and Borätt (CABE 2010).

KEY POLICY AND DESIGN MEASURES

The integration of transportation and land use planning was recognized as a key component affecting the sustainability of the project. Expansion of the district has been complemented by transportation investments, including increased bus service, bicycle paths, pedestrian bridges, ferry service and an extension of the tram line. Development has been focused on a dense settlement structure, concentrated along main transit corridors. In order to discourage car use, parking in the area is limited and is priced. Key policy and design strategies applied are described below.

Public transportation

Substantial investments were made in public transportation in the area, including an extension of the Tvärbanan tram line (Line 22), which runs through Hammarby Sjöstad with four stops in the district. The line operates all day from 5:30 a.m. to 1:00 a.m. This orbital line incorporates several features that enhance quality of service, including level boarding at stations, which allows easier access to the trains, and message boards providing real-time arrival information of the next trains. In addition to the tram line, two bus routes serve the area.

The Tvärbanan tram line is particularly important to residents as one-third of trips made by residents are on this line alone (Brick 2008). Figure 5.2 shows a dramatic growth in ridership on the Tvärbanan line after the introduction of the central Stockholm congestion charge in 2006 (see Box 5.2). Hammarby Sjöstad lies just outside of the central Stockholm congestion zone. This increase in ridership demonstrates the effect that integrating measures (such as congestion pricing and improved public transit service) can

5: STOCKHOLM: HAMMARBY SJÖSTAD CASE STUDY

Photo 5.4

Residential mixed use in Hammarby Sjöstad

Source: Photo by Simon Field

have on the behavior of travelers, increasing the potential to shift travelers from cars to more sustainable modes such as public transit.

In addition, the Gullmarsplan Tunnelbanan (metro) station lies just outside the boarder of Hammarby Sjöstad. This station serves the T17, T18 and T19 metro lines and provides direct service to central Stockholm at seven- to eight-minute frequencies during peak hours. The station also serves as a multimodal transfer facility with connections to the Tvärbanan tram line and numerous bus lines.

In addition to providing convenient access, fare structure can also help drive public transportation use. Public transportation tickets in Stockholm County are integrated and zone-based. The same ticket can be used on the bus, tram or metro, improving ease of transfers. Several ticket options are offered from single tickets to annual travel cards, all with both regular and reduced prices. Stockholm has an integrated smartcard called SL Access. Transit tickets and passes can be loaded onto this smartcard. An SL Business Card is also available for employees of participating companies. Through this program, the employee is given a travel card at a discounted price, and the cost is deducted from his or her salary; the employer pays social security contributions. This is a way for companies to encourage employees to use public transit. Passengers may also purchase tickets on mobile phones. The ticket will appear on the mobile phone screen and must be shown to the bus operator upon boarding (http://sl.se/).

A ferry service was introduced that transports passengers from Hammarby Sjöstad to the Stockholm city center and to Sodermalm, an island located between Hammarby Sjöstad and the city center. More

Photo 5.5

Tvärbanan line tram stop in Hammarby Sjöstad

Source: Photo by Carleton Wong

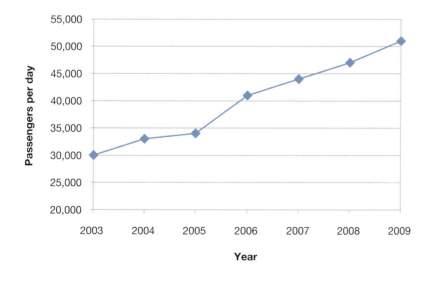

Figure 5.2

Ridership on Tvärbanan line

> **BOX 5.2 STOCKHOLM CONGESTION CHARGE**
>
> The City of Stockholm has successfully implemented a congestion charge in the city center with the primary objectives of reducing congestion, increasing accessibility and improving the environment. Similar schemes have also been implemented in London, Singapore and several cities in Norway. In Stockholm, charges are tallied as drivers enter the toll area either by reading a transponder that drivers can attach to their vehicles or by photos taken of vehicle license plates.
>
> As a complement to the charge and in order to encourage a shift from driving to public transit use, before the trial, Stockholm invested nearly $180 million in public transit improvements. Sixteen new bus lines serving the inner city were added and the frequency on existing routes was increased.
>
> The trial was successful in reducing traffic congestion and increasing public transit use. During the trial period, the road traffic volume across the cordon decreased by 22 percent. Nearly 100,000 vehicles were removed during peak business hours each day. There was also a 30–50 percent reduction of travel time, which was even greater than what was expected. The percentage of those traveling by public transit increased by 4 percent and many work trips were shifted from car to public transit.
>
> The trial also had a significant impact on improving the environmental quality of the city. CO_2 emissions were reduced by 40 percent in the inner city and emissions of nitrogen oxide, particulate matter and other noxious pollutants declined by 8–14 percent in the inner city. Furthermore, it is estimated that the reduced exposure to particles will lead to a 25–30 percent reduction in premature deaths per year.
>
> At the beginning of this trial, 55 percent of Stockholm residents did not agree with the charge. However, after realizing the great benefits offered by this charging system, public opinion swung in favor of it. A referendum on the continued implementation of the congestion charge was held during the general election in 2006. Voters reaffirmed their support to reinstate the congestion pricing scheme and the new government decided to make the congestion charge permanent from 2007 on.

information about these two ferry lines is summarized in Table 5.1. Ferry service is run by the City of Stockholm. Bicycles can be taken on board all ferries and ferry terminals are located near bicycle lanes, providing an easy transition between bike and ferry. Studies have suggested that introduction of the ferry service has contributed to an increase in the use of bicycles and walking to/from Hammarby Sjöstad and that as much as 24 percent of travelers use the ferry for some portion of their trip (Brick 2008).

Bicycle and pedestrian infrastructure

One goal was for Hammarby Sjöstad to be a healthy place for people to live; that offers opportunities for exercise, sports and culture. Integrated into this goal was the construction of numerous bike paths, pedestrian paths and footbridges. Many of the paths provide an opportunity for scenic strolls along picturesque canals and through a variety of green spaces. The bicycle lanes also enable improved mobility, running along thoroughfares such as Lugnets Allé and Hammarby Allé. Providing safe, accessible bicycle

5: STOCKHOLM: HAMMARBY SJÖSTAD CASE STUDY

Photo 5.6

Ferry terminal in Hammarby Sjöstad

Source: Photo by Carleton Wong

Table 5.1 Summary of Hammarby Sjöstad ferry service

Ferry destination	Travel time to destination	Frequency	Hours of operation	Operating months	Cost
Sodermalm	5 minutes	10–15 minutes	06:00 to midnight	Year round	Free
Nybroviken (Central Stockholm)	25 minutes	1 hour	Weekdays: 07:30–17:30 Weekends: 09:30–18:30	May 31– October 1	Regular fare: $5 Discount fare: $3 Children under 13: free

Source: City of Stockholm

and pedestrian infrastructure is important to both encourage healthy activities, but also to promote use of non-motorized forms of transportation.

Bike sharing

The bike sharing program in Stockholm, called Stockholm City Bikes, was implemented in 2006 and is operated by Clear Channel Communications, whose outdoor advertising unit is specialized in bike rental services worldwide. The company holds similar bike sharing programs in France (Rennes, Caen, Dijon and Perpignan), as well as in Barcelona, Oslo, Milan and Mexico City.

In Stockholm, as of July 2015, there were 1,800 bikes and 140 docking stations, four of which were located in Hammarby Sjöstad. At each station, spaces for nine to 24 bicycles are available. The actual number of bikes available at any time depends on the number currently in use and the bicycle distribution patterns of users. Once the program is fully implemented, there will be 2,500 bicycles at 200 locations throughout Stockholm (http://citybikes.se/home).

Unlike typical renting conditions in other European cities, loaning a bike in Stockholm is only possible from April to October. The bikes may be picked up between 6:00 a.m. and 10:00 p.m. while returning a bike is not subject to any time limit, in order to ensure broad access, a user cannot loan a bike for

5: STOCKHOLM: HAMMARBY SJÖSTAD CASE STUDY

Photo 5.7 *(top left)*

Tree-lined pedestrian pathway in Hammarby Sjöstad

Source: Photo by Carleton Wong

Photo 5.8 *(top right)*

Pedestrian bridge in Hammarby Sjöstad

Source: Photo by Carleton Wong

Photo 5.9 *(right)*

Pedestrian walkways along canal in Hammarby Sjöstad

Source: Photo by Adrienne Miller

5: STOCKHOLM: HAMMARBY SJÖSTAD CASE STUDY

more than three hours or will have to pay a penalty. A membership and rental card are required for use. Two types of cards are available. A seasonal card may be purchased online for approximately $30 or at a retailer for $35. A three-day card must be purchased at a retailer and costs around $20 (City of Stockholm). There is also an option to add a Stockholm City Bike membership to an SL Access smartcard.

Carsharing

Carsharing is a strategy that has been shown to be successful in reducing car ownership rates and vehicle miles traveled. Users have access to a car without having to own one. There are currently more than 40 low emissions carsharing cars with dedicated parking spaces located in Hammarby Sjöstad, belonging to three different carsharing organizations: Sunfleet Carsharing, Bilpoolen and CityCarClub.

Car2Go, the one-way or point-to-point carsharing company, is also in operation in the City of Stockholm.

According to a survey of residents in 2010, 18 percent of households had a carsharing membership (ITDP 2010). In 2008, 100 companies located in Hammarby Sjöstad were reported as having a carsharing membership (City of Stockholm).

Parking

Limiting the parking supply helps discourage car use and encourage use of alternative modes of travel. In addition, having less land dedicated to parking means there is more land available for other uses.

Photo 5.10 (left)

Bike-sharing station in Hammarby Sjöstad

Source: Photo by Carleton Wong

Photo 5.11 (right)

Carsharing vehicle in Hammarby Sjöstad

Source: Photo by Adrienne Miller

5: STOCKHOLM: HAMMARBY SJÖSTAD CASE STUDY

Photo 5.12

Car2Go vehicle in Stockholm

Source: Photo by Carleton Wong

Photo 5.13

Parking signage in Hammarby Sjöstad

Source: Photo by Carleton Wong

Hammarby Sjöstad has approximately 0.15 on-street parking spaces per household, and an estimated 0.55 spaces per household in public or private garages. The supply of parking is not evenly spread, and in some parts of the district the practical parking supply will be much lower. Overall, Hammarby Sjöstad has 0.65 parking spaces per household.

Charging for parking is another important strategy to limit car use. On-street parking in Hammarby Sjöstad is regulated in the same way as for the rest of the inner city. Parking is charged between 9:00 a.m. and 5:00 p.m. on weekdays. Evening and nighttime parking is free. Off-street parking is mainly operated by Stockholm Parkering, the city's parking company, which owns a number of garages and off-street parking lots in Hammarby Sjöstad. Additionally, a number of the housing cooperatives own their own parking and set their own prices for residents, and there are also a few private parking garage operators. Table 5.2

Table 5.2 Parking prices in Hammarby Sjöstad

Time period	On-street parking	Off-street outdoor parking	Off-street garage parking
Per hour	$1.75	$1.50–$1.75	$2.30
Per day (24 hours)	$5.85*	$7–$10	$12
Overnight	-	-	$7
Monthly	$82*	$88	$130–$175
Yearly	$980*	$1,050	$1,540–$2,100

* With residential parking permit

Source: City of Stockholm, Traffic Administration

shows the parking prices for Stockholm Parkering. The prices for off-street parking are comparable to other areas just outside the inner city, but a little lower than typical prices inside the inner city.

One important aspect is that typically parking management strategies encourage charging more for on-street parking spaces than for off-street spaces. This encourages long-term parkers to park off-street and maintains a larger number of on-street spaces available for short-term parkers, who have a faster turnover. Hammarby Sjöstad's parking pricing structure does not follow this strategy, and it is recommended to raise on-street parking prices.

Urban design

The layout of Hammarby Sjöstad was designed to integrate transportation, amenities and public spaces. The spine of the district is a 125-foot-wide boulevard and transit corridor, which connects key transport nodes and public focal points, and creates a natural focus for activity and commerce.

Street layout and design

Two main thoroughfares, Lugnets Allé and Hammarby Allé, run through the district. These streets consist of tram lines in the middle of the street with boarding platforms on the outside. Beyond the boarding platforms, there is one car lane in each direction, and outside the car lanes are bicycle lanes followed by parking spaces and then pedestrian walkways. The bike lanes are painted on the street, and in some locations cars must pass over the bike lane in order to park. Pedestrian priority is given on the main streets, complemented by speed restrictions and frequent zebra crossings.

Public space design

A network of varied parks, green spaces, quays and walkways runs through the district, providing space for outdoor activities. All public spaces are owned and maintained by the City of Stockholm. The initial goal for the development was to provide 270 square feet of public green space per apartment unit, for a total of 3.2 million square feet in the district. So far, a total of 3 million square feet have been completed. The development also has a goal to provide 160 square feet of private courtyard space per apartment unit (City of Stockholm).

Land use planning and design

The general building layout of Hammarby Sjöstad is blocks built around an inner courtyard. The entire development is high-density, but with the highest densities focused along the transit corridor, where buildings are seven to eight stories high. The average height of buildings in the district is 60 feet, or six stories. Safety on the streets is enhanced by providing a variety of ground floor uses, and facing balconies and front doors onto the street in order to increase "eyes on the street." The architectural style utilizes contemporary sustainability technologies and follows modern architectural principles, maximizing use of daylight and providing views of water and green spaces.

Photo 5.14

Waterfront walkway in Hammarby Sjöstad

Source: Photo by Adrienne Miller

Photo 5.15

Cafe in Hammarby Sjöstad

Source: Photo by Luc Nadal

The residential units include a mix of tenures; 46 percent of the units are rented and 54 percent are owned. Most of the apartment units have one or two bedrooms, as seen in Table 5.3. In addition, the development has 59 apartments with 24-hour care for the elderly, 30 apartment units where assisted residential care is provided and 400 student flats.

Table 5.3 Breakdown of residential unit size in Hammarby Sjöstad

Studios	9%
1 bedrooms	35%
2 bedrooms	32%
3 bedrooms	21%
4 bedrooms	2%
5+ bedrooms	< 1%

Source: City of Stockholm

BOX 5.3 STOCKHOLM DISABILITY PROGRAM

In 2004, the Stockholm Local Council adopted the Disability Policy Program whose aim was to make Stockholm the most accessible city in the world by 2010. To reach this goal, the document enlists a series of wide scale measures to be undertaken. In the transportation sector, the program recommends removing all physical barriers that can easily be removed. This includes widening doorways and installing handrails in public transit stations and providing level boarding of transit vehicles. The program also stipulates that all public authorities and private companies need to integrate financing of these measures into their budgets. The goal is to provide better access to disabled persons and, consequently, enhance democracy and social equity among all Stockholmers. Due to its goal of becoming an exemplary district for the future, Hammarby Sjöstad has paid special attention to satisfying these requirements (Disability Policy Programme for the City of Stockholm 2005).

The planning department recognized the importance of providing a mix of uses in order to ensure that residents have access to goods and services within walking distance. Therefore, the city initially offered a two-year rent-free subsidy in order to attract commercial operators and to ensure that service provision was established during the early phases of the development (CABE 2010). This strategy was successful, and today the area includes nearly 100 retail units and restaurants, as well as office space and light industrial uses, employing over 5,000 people. In addition, at least five food stores are located throughout the development and no one lives more than half a mile from a grocery store. The mix of uses in Hammarby Sjöstad includes the following institutional uses: 12 preschools, three primary schools, two high schools, a library, a cultural center, a chapel, an environmental center, child-care facilities and healthcare centers (City of Stockholm).

Sustainable use of resources

Sustainable use of resources has also been an important focus for Hammarby Sjöstad. The integrated environmental solutions can be followed through an eco-cycle that has become known as the Hammarby Model (Figure 5.3). This model, developed by Fortum and the Stockholm Water Company, incorporates sewage processing, energy provision and waste handling in order to maximize reuse of recycled materials and conversion of waste into energy that can be used by the development.

Waste is sorted and deposited by residents at specified refuse stations. Biogas is extracted from organic waste and used to provide district heating and electricity, and to fuel inner-city buses, garbage trucks and taxis. The district has a fuel station for cars running on electricity, biogas or ethanol. Waste that is not to be reused is transported through vacuum tubes to pick-up stations outside the development to reduce distance traveled by garbage trucks—both decreasing truck emissions and reducing the need for garbage trucks to enter the district.

Building features applied in order to save energy include extra heat insulation, energy-efficient windows, on-demand ventilation, individual metering of heating and hot water in apartments, energy-

5: STOCKHOLM: HAMMARBY SJÖSTAD CASE STUDY

Figure 5.3

The Hammarby Model

Source: Glashus Ett

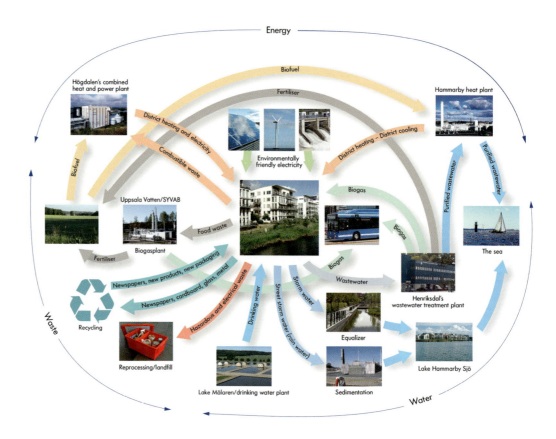

efficient appliances, lighting controls, solar cells, solar panels and fuel cells. The solar cells are particularly efficient, yielding as much as 50 percent of the annual hot tap water requirement. Some of the buildings have installed heat pumps and heat exchangers for air ventilation. The use of energy-efficient building features along with renewable energy sources has resulted in a reduction in energy demand from 100 to 60 kilowatt hours per square meter per year. In order to conserve water, the developers have installed low-flow shower heads and reduced-flush toilets. Emphasis was also placed on the use of eco-friendly building materials (Brick 2008).

Experience from Hammarby Sjöstad's innovative approach to sustainable resource use is now being applied to all local planning in Stockholm (Stockholms Stad 2008).

QUANTITATIVE COMPARISON

In order to quantify the benefits of the sustainability measures implemented in Hammarby Sjöstad, it is important to look at the development in the context of its location. Hammarby Sjöstad is located in one of the most progressive cities in the world with regard to sustainability. Stockholm was the winner of the European Green Capital City competition for 2010. The city reduced carbon emissions by 25 percent per resident between 1990 and 2010, and has established targets for reducing per capita CO_2 emissions. In 2010, the emissions rate for the city was just over four tons of CO_2 per capita. This value is extremely low for developed countries, considering the entire country of Sweden had an average emission rate of seven tons of CO_2 per capita in 2010, the average for Europe was nine tons per capita and the average for the United States was 22 tons per capita (EIA 2009).

The City of Stockholm has recognized the connection between land use planning and transportation and has taken many measures to steer development in the direction of a dense settlement structure, complemented by investments in public transportation, bicycling and pedestrian infrastructure. Furthermore, the city has successfully implemented a city center congestion charge.

Table 5.4 Statistics for Hammarby Sjöstad, Sundbyberg, Inner Stockholm and City of Stockholm

	Hammarby Sjöstad	Sundbyberg	Inner City Stockholm	City of Stockholm
Population	20,000	37,700	310,000	830,000
Area (Acres)	400	2,200	8,600	46,000
Population density (persons/acre)	50	17	36	18
Average annual income	$42,000	$32,000	N/A	$34,000
Jobs per resident	0.3	0.5	N/A	N/A
Cars per 1,000 residents	210	295	N/A	370
Car parking spaces/ residential unit	0.65	N/A	0.65	0.65
Mode share for all trips				
Car	21%	44%	17%	32%
Public transit	52%	20%	36%	30%
Bicycle/walking	27%	36%	47%	38%

Sources: City of Stockholm, City of Sundbyberg (www.sundbyberg.se/), Blomquist (2010), ITDP (2010)

Density

Hammarby Sjöstad's statistics are impressive even when compared to this ambitious setting. Compared to both the inner city of Stockholm and the City of Stockholm itself, Hammarby Sjöstad has a higher population density, as seen in Table 5.4. The provision of on-street parking is lower for Hammarby Sjöstad than for the city; however, the provision of off-street parking is higher, bringing the total to 0.65 spaces per residential unit for both Hammarby Sjöstad and the city as a whole.

Car ownership rates

Hammarby Sjöstad is also compared to the municipality of Sundbyberg, which is located three miles to the northwest of the Stockholm city center and also has good public transit connections. Car ownership per resident is quite low in Sundbyberg (295 cars per 1,000 residents) and is even lower in Hammarby Sjöstad (210 cars per 1,000 residents). These values are both smaller than for the City of Stockholm (370 cars per 1,000 residents), which is already low by international standards in developed countries. These and other statistics are summarized in Table 5.4. In addition, bicycle ownership is quite high in Hammarby Sjöstad at 820 bikes per 1,000 residents (ITDP 2010).

Mode split

The policy and design measures employed in Hammarby Sjöstad have proven effective. Only 21 percent of trips made by Hammarby Sjöstad residents are by car, while 52 percent are by public transportation, and 27 percent by non-motorized modes. The percentage of non-motorized trips (27 percent) is still not quite as high as for those in Sundbyberg (36 percent), Inner City Stockholm (47 percent) or the city as a whole (38 percent), as seen in Figure 5.4. This may be due to the high concentration of jobs in Sundbyberg and Inner Stockholm, making it possible for residents of these areas to bike or walk to work nearby. However, compared to a reference district without integrated policy and design measures, Hammarby Sjöstad has a higher percentage of trips made by bike (9 percent) and on foot (18 percent) than the reference district's share of bike trips (7 percent) and walking trips (8 percent), as seen in Figure 5.5.

5: STOCKHOLM: HAMMARBY SJÖSTAD CASE STUDY

Figure 5.4

Transportation mode split for various regions in Stockholm County

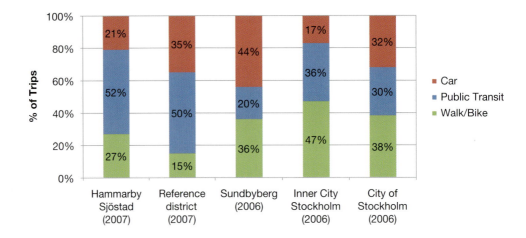

Figure 5.5

Transportation mode split for Hammarby Sjöstad and reference district (2007)

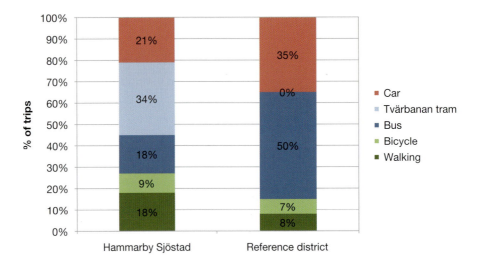

In addition, Hammarby Sjöstad has a much higher share of trips made by public transit (52 percent) than Sundbyberg (20 percent), Inner City Stockholm (36 percent) or the city as a whole (30 percent). This demonstrates that although residents of Sundbyberg walk or bike for more trips than Hammarby Sjöstad residents, for motorized trips residents of Hammarby Sjöstad choose public transit over the car for a far greater percentage of trips than Sundbyberg residents. The breakdown of mode split for the regions discussed can be seen in Figure 5.4. Figure 5.5 shows a more detailed breakdown of mode split for Hammarby Sjöstad and a reference district. The Hammarby Sjöstad values are generated from questionnaire-based surveys of residents. The reference district values are based on a previous overall study of comparable city districts, but have been adapted for Hammarby Sjöstad (Brick 2008).

Furthermore, an Internet-based survey of Hammarby Sjöstad residents conducted by ITDP in 2010 asked respondents what mode of transportation they take most often to get to work. It was found that 3 percent of respondents walk to work, 14 percent bike, 78 percent take public transit and 5 percent drive, as seen in Figure 5.6. This shows that residents overwhelmingly prefer to take public transportation to work rather than driving. Stockholm's congestion charge likely has an influence on this decision. In addition, the survey found that 39 percent of residents live less than three miles from their place of work, 43 percent live between three and six miles, and 18 percent live more than six miles from work. These short commute distances also make it easy to travel to work by non-motorized modes or public transit. The average one-way commute time of residents was found to be 33 minutes (ITDP 2010).

5: STOCKHOLM: HAMMARBY SJÖSTAD CASE STUDY

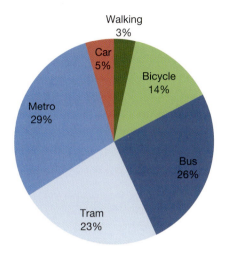

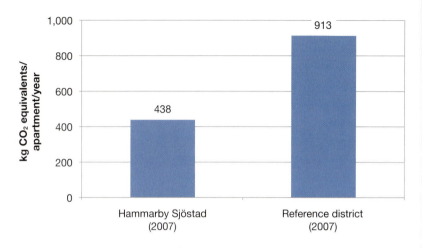

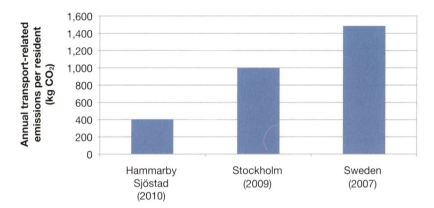

Figure 5.6 (top left)

Mode of travel to work, Hammarby Sjöstad residents (2010)

Figure 5.7 (top right)

Comparison of car emissions for Hammarby Sjöstad and reference district

Figure 5.8 (left)

Comparison of transport-related emissions for residents of Hammarby Sjöstad, Stockholm and Sweden

Transport-related emissions

The low car ownership rate, low car mode share and short commute distances help to reduce the carbon footprint of Hammarby Sjöstad residents. CO_2 emissions per apartment from personal transport by car are more than 50 percent lower in Hammarby Sjöstad than in the reference district, as seen in Figure 5.7. These savings alone would yield a reduction of approximately 2,600 tons of CO2 per year (Brick 2008).

Moreover, by measuring miles traveled per resident per year by both private and public transport, along with estimates of emission rates of vehicles, it is estimated that overall transport-related emissions for residents of Hammarby Sjöstad are less than half that for an average Stockholm resident and less than a third that of an average resident of Sweden, as seen in Figure 5.8.

The statistics presented in this section quantify some of the many benefits of integrated policy and design measures. These comparisons show that even in a city as ambitious as Stockholm, concentration of integrated policy and design measures in a single district can bring about further reductions in carbon footprint.

LESSONS LEARNED

A holistic approach to planning, grounded in strong environmental goals, can help shape better new developments. These goals should be created as early as possible, making it possible to integrate the environmental profile in every part of the infrastructure early in the urban district planning process. The process of formulating goals should be done in close cooperation with all stakeholders and should include a discussion of possible technical solutions and their potential results within the planned district.

Context is also important to new developments. In Stockholm, the availability of high-quality transportation alternatives and the congestion charge have a strong influence on residents, including those in this new development.

The planning process should keep in mind that the environmental profile does not end once the development is built. The district plan should include information and incentive components to influence the behavior and commitment of residents to ensure that the ideals and goals of the plan continue even after the district is built. Following this line of thought, new urban districts should design an evaluation process with a structure for follow-up with a clearly defined feedback process to ensure continued sustainability of the project.

Our next case study is also located in Sweden and was planned around the same time as Hammarby Sjöstad. Västra Hamnen, in Malmö, was similarly envisioned to be a driving force in Sweden's development toward environmental sustainability.

REFERENCES

Blomquist, A. (2010) *Fakta om SL och Lanet 2009*, Stockholm: AB Storstockholms Lokaltrafik.
Brick, K. (2008) *Report Summary: Follow Up of Environmental Impact in Hammarby Sjöstad*, Stockholm: Grontmij AB.
CABE (Commission for Architecture and the Built Environment), Hammarby Sjöstad Case Study, 2010, United Kingdom.
Cervero, R. and Sullivan, C. (2010) *Toward Green TODs*, Working Paper UCB-ITS-VWP-2010-7, UC Berkeley Center for Future Urban Transport, Berkeley, CA.
Disability Policy Programme for the City of Stockholm: Summarized Version (2005), Malmö.
City of Sundbyberg, www.sundbyberg.se/.
Communication with Björn Cederquist, City Planning Department, City of Stockholm, June 2015.
Communication with Daniel Firth, Transport Planner, Stockholm City Traffic Administration, June 2015.
Communication with Malena Karlsson, GlashusEtt—the center for environmental information and communication in Hammarby Sjöstad, July 2010.
EIA (2009), *Carbon Emissions from Consumption of Energy*, available at: www.guardian.co.uk/environment/data blog/2009/dec/07/copenhagen-climate-change-summit-carbon-emissions-data-country-world (accessed July 2010).
Fränne, L. (2007) *Hammarby Sjöstad: A Unique Environmental Project in Stockholm*, Stockholm: GlashusEtt.
Hall, S. P. (1998) *Cities in Civilization*, New York: Random House.
ITDP (2010) Internet-based survey of Hammarby Sjöstad residents.
Stockholms Stad (2008) *The Stockholm Environment Programme 2008–2011: Overarching Goals and Priorities*, Stockholm: Stockholms Stad.

6
Malmö
Västra Hamnen case study

BACKGROUND

All of the low carbon communities studied are ambitious and intentional, but among the case studies Malmö is perhaps the most aggressive at becoming an internationally leading example of environmental adaptation of a densely built urban district. For example, the centerpiece of the project is the 54-story Turning Torso tower, designed by renowned "starchitect" Santiago Calatrava. The tower stands out in an area of otherwise mid-rise development, and draws attention to the development in a way that the other prior case studies do not, instead blending into the surrounding neighborhoods, leading to debates about the efficacy and necessity of high-rise towers. The rest of the development is architecturally interesting while still not losing sight of the goal of reducing car dependence.

Västra Hamnen is a brownfield redevelopment that provides a mix of uses, high-quality bicycling and pedestrian infrastructure, good transit access and carsharing, and places an emphasis on mobility management. Non-motorized transportation use is higher and car use is lower in Västra Hamnen than in the city as a whole. An overarching ecological approach to planning, building and construction was a key tool in the creation of the district.

Västra Hamnen (the western harbor) has, in a couple of decades, been transformed from an industrial park into a lively district focused on knowledge and sustainable living. Since the closing of Kockums Machine Halls, the district has become home to new parks, swimming areas, business campuses, schools

Photo 6.1

Plaza in Västra Hamnen

Source: Photo by Kristofer Steimer

**BOX 6.1
VÄSTRA HAMNEN
SITE FACTS**

Developer:
Multiple

Architect:
Multiple[1]

Population:
7,000

Projected population:
20,000

Developed area:
215 acres

Total area:
430 acres

Current density:
33 persons/acre

Projected density:
47 persons/acre

Current residential units:
4,000

Planned residential units:
11,000

Construction began:
1998

Planned completion:
2031

Distance from city center:
1.2 miles

Cars:
440 cars/1,000 residents

Non-motorized mode share:
60%

Public transport mode share:
17%

Residents with carsharing:
3%

1 Over 20 architects have been involved; some of the most notable architects include Klas Tham, Ralph Erskine and Santiago Calatrava.

6: MALMÖ: VÄSTRA HAMNEN CASE STUDY

and residences. The Västra Hamnen campus of Malmö University opened in 1998, and three years later was the opening of the European Home Fair for Bo01. These two milestones marked the beginning of a new urban district coming to life in Malmö.

Bo01 was the first development stage of the Västra Hamnen regeneration project. The vision for Bo01 was to create a new and modern mixed-use neighborhood, committed to sustainable principles. The development was built as part of the European Housing Expo 2001, themed "City of Tomorrow." The 350 residential units presented at the expo were comprised of a mix of tenures and were built following a set of guidelines for architectural quality, choice of materials, energy consumption, sustainable transportation, green issues and technical infrastructure. Since its completion, its legacy has been applied to other neighborhoods in Västra Hamnen, which have also been constructed following ecological guidelines and incorporating a sustainability focus.

As mentioned, the most distinctive visual icon of Västra Hamnen is the Turning Torso tower, designed by Spanish architect Santiago Calatrava. It consists of nine rotating cubes containing 54 floors, accommodating offices at the bottom, conference facilities at the top, and in between 147 apartments, twisting 90 degrees from top to bottom, with a rooftop observation deck. At nearly 625 feet, it is the tallest building in the Nordic countries and one of the tallest residential buildings in the European Union.

Västra Hamnen has received international acclaim, both for its innovative sustainability features and its striking architecture. It demonstrates that modern development can both be environmentally conscious and attractive.

PLANNING PROCESS

Beginning in the late 1800s, Västra Hamnen was primarily used as a port and industrial area, and was home to the Kockums shipyard. By the late 1970s, the shipping industry began to decline, and in 1979 the Swedish government took over Kockums Machine Halls. By the 1990s, the city's vision for the area began to move away from industrial activities. The City of Malmö recognized the district's potential as an attractive waterfront area, located close to the city center, and decided to convert this once industrial zone into a new urbanized district with a focus on education and sustainable living. It was decided, in connection with Malmö City's Vision Project in 1994/95, to locate a new campus of Malmö University in Västra Hamnen. The university opened in 1998 (Malmö Stad 2009a).

The city also decided to build an eco-village that could be seen as an international example of sustainable development. The Bo01 project, termed "City of Tomorrow," was showcased at the 2001 European Housing Expo. The primary investors in Bo01 were the national government, the City of Malmö and Sydkraft (a regional power company). The City of Malmö received money from the national government through a local investment program, covering environmental measures in Bo01. This money was used for technical systems, soil decontamination, infrastructure and educational projects. The European Union also gave financial support for energy-efficiency measures. As a result, it was required that a scientific evaluation be made in order to capitalize on Malmö's experience in sustainable urban development and share lessons learned with future projects both locally and internationally. Ongoing research is still being conducted on topics as diverse as soil decontamination, traffic, mobility management, energy

Photo 6.2 *(facing page, top)*
Public walkways in Västra Hamnen
Source: Photo by La Citta Vita on Flickr

Photo 6.3 *(facing page, bottom)*
Turning Torso in Västra Hamnen
Source: Photo by Kristofer Steimer

6: MALMÖ: VÄSTRA HAMNEN CASE STUDY

Figure 6.1

Map of Västra Hamnen

Source: Map by Amy Smith

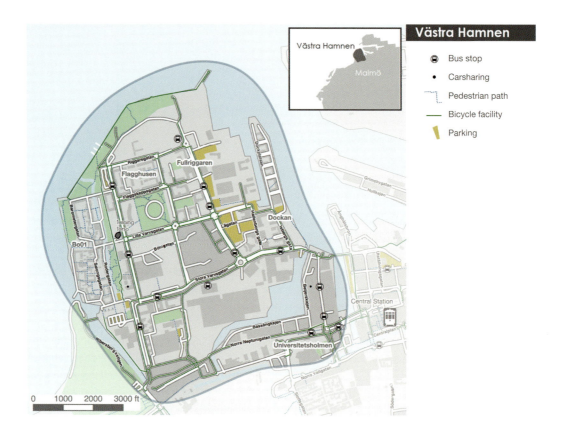

efficiency, green structure, storm water reuse, recycling and sustainable development (Malmö Stad 2015).

Expansion of Bo01 continued after the housing expo, including construction of the district's landmark, the Turning Torso tower. The city authorities regarded a tall building in this location as important in terms of giving Malmö a new landmark, and therefore granted the scheme planning permission.

Beyond Bo01, other neighborhoods have been developed at Västra Hamnen, including the residential neighborhoods of Dockan, Fullriggaren and Flagghusen and the University District of Universitetsholmen (Figure 6.1). These developments incorporate high-density residential units with businesses, schools, service facilities, parks and recreational facilities. So far, approximately 215 of the total 430 acres have been developed. Plans for the district include additional residential neighborhoods, in addition to blocks dedicated to education and training facilities, a conference center and concert hall, and office buildings. All of these development projects are being undertaken with a focus on sustainability. The district is planned to eventually house 20,000 residents and provide 17,000 jobs (Malmö Stad 2015).

New approaches to the planning process are continuing to be implemented, such as the "sustainability dialogue" that was tested during the planning of the Flagghusen residential area, which consists of 16 buildings and more than 600 apartment units. Planning of this development included a dialogue between citizens and the developer in order to develop the best solutions for those involved. Important concerns were safety and security, affordability, architecture, planning issues, parking, energy efficiency, the environment and quality. As a result, Flagghusen has set new standards for social, economic and ecological sustainability, demonstrating that Västra Hamnen is continuing to push forward as a modern example of sustainable development (Malmö Stad 2015).

KEY POLICY AND DESIGN MEASURES

Västra Hamnen was planned to minimize future transportation needs and car dependency. There are 260 miles of bicycle paths throughout the City of Malmö, which prides itself on being one of the world's leading bicycling cities. In Västra Hamnen alone, there are more than five miles of new bicycle paths.

In addition, many improvements have been made in Västra Hamnen in order to make public transportation more attractive. Buses connecting central parts of Malmö with vital areas of Västra Hamnen have been increased and transit-only lanes have been added. These and other policy and design strategies, discussed below, aim to reduce car dependency of residents and make Västra Hamnen a quality place to live.

Sustainable mobility report

In 2012, the City of Malmo introduced a Traffic Environment Program, which set goals to reduce the share of trips made by cars. The program set a goal of reducing the car mode share of all trips made by Malmo residents from 41 percent to 30 percent by 2030, and to reduce the car mode share of incoming commuters from 67 percent to 50 percent by 2030. Following this, Västra Hamnen released a sustainable mobility in Västra Hamnen report, setting even stricter goals for the neighborhood itself than were set by the city. The goal for Västra Hamnen residents is to have a car mode share of 25 percent or lower and a 30 percent car mode share for incoming commuters to Västra Hamnen by 2030 (Camilla Morland, pers. comm.).

The sustainable mobility in Västra Hamnen report prioritizes walking, biking and public transit, and stresses the role of education and marketing to shift behavior. The following are policies described in the report that would help facilitate reaching the mobility goals set for the neighborhood:

- communicate the city's policy regarding traffic;
- provide mobility management projects to both companies and residents;
- develop informational material for visitors about sustainable travel;
- assist developers in getting environmental certification;
- prioritize bicycle travel;
- facilitate safe, efficient pedestrian travel;
- provide fast, high-capacity public transit;
- implement traffic-calming measures; and
- implement parking management strategies.

Bicycle and pedestrian infrastructure

Västra Hamnen has a focus on promoting biking and walking. Bicyclists and pedestrians are given priority in the Bo01 neighborhood and the area is primarily car-free. Bicycle and pedestrian paths are incorporated throughout the Västra Hamnen district, including more than five miles of new bicycle paths.

A long bicycle route runs through Malmö from the southern part of the inner city to Universitetsholmen, the university district in Västra Hamnen. A variety of innovative features are being tested along this stretch, aimed at improving bicycle safety and ease of use. These solutions include rails at traffic lights that bicyclists can rest against so that they do not need to put their foot down, and mirrors placed at low-visibility intersections so that bicyclists can see what is happening around the corner. Different types of lighting will be tested along the route to improve nighttime visibility. In addition,

6: MALMÖ: VÄSTRA HAMNEN CASE STUDY

Photo 6.4

Mothers walking in pedestrian space in Västra Hamnen

Source: Photo by La Citta Vita on Flickr

Photo 6.5

People walking and biking near waterfront in Västra Hamnen

Source: Photo by La Citta Vita on Flickr

several mini service stations have been set up where bicyclists can pump air into their tires and carry out simple repairs.

The City of Malmö has even given bicyclists priority at more than 30 traffic lights across the city. Radar sensors have been fitted at these crossings to detect approaching bicyclists and give them a green light. This allows bicyclists to flow more smoothly in traffic and clearly demonstrates the city's commitment to promoting bicycling (Malmö Stad 2009b).

6: MALMÖ: VÄSTRA HAMNEN CASE STUDY

Photo 6.6

Bus in bus-only lane in Västra Hamnen

Public transportation

Västra Hamnen is well served by transit. At least one bus stop is located within 1,000 feet of every apartment, and buses run at seven-minute intervals throughout the day. Many investments have been made to improve the quality of public transportation in the area. Buses are given high priority at traffic lights in order to speed up service, and to reduce boarding times passengers may board through all doors of the bus. Red bus-only lanes run through Västra Hamnen and other parts of the city. Bus stops have elevated platforms to make boarding faster and easier, and many stops now have weather protection to make waiting more comfortable. In addition, stops across the city are equipped with electronic timetables so passengers know how long they must wait for the next bus to arrive. Real-time bus arrival information is also available through mobile phone apps.

From the southern border of Västra Hamnen, it is just over half a mile, an easy five-minute bike ride, to Malmö Central Station. This station connects to the Øresund Bridge through the new City Tunnel, which links train travel north of the city to regional connection points, including Copenhagen. The City Tunnel consists of 10 miles of railway and four miles of tunnel, representing the largest investment in public transport in Malmö's history (Øresundsbro Konsortiet 2009).

Public transportation in Malmö is run by Skånetrafiken, the regional public transportation authority and operator in southern Sweden. Skånetrafiken uses a zone-based fare system with integrated tickets between different transport modes and for travel between southern Sweden and Denmark. In 2009, Skånetrafiken introduced a contactless smartcard called "Jojo." Patrons can load transit tickets, monthly travel passes and discount travel cards onto this smartcard. Children pay a discounted price, and discounts are also available for family members traveling together. In addition, bus tickets can be purchased and displayed on mobile phones (www.skanetrafiken.se/).

Efforts have also been made to reduce emissions from buses. In 2003, a pilot project was launched in which two city buses operating in the area were fueled by a mixture of 8 percent hydrogen gas from wind power and 92 percent vehicle fuel (Malmö Stad 2009a). The project was very successful and now a majority of buses in the city use this fuel mixture.

Parking

The planners of Västra Hamnen have recognized the importance of limiting parking in order to reduce car use; however, implementation of this strategy has been somewhat of a challenge. Initially, parking

> **BOX 6.2** THE ØRESUND BRIDGE
>
> The world-famous Øresund Bridge connects the metropolitan areas of Copenhagen in Denmark and Malmö in Sweden over the Øresund Strait. Primarily orchestrated by architect Georg K. S. Rotne, the link carries two rail tracks and four car lanes. The official inauguration took place on July 1, 2000, after seven years of construction work. In 2009 alone, 15.1 million passengers crossed the bridge by car and 11.2 million by train.
>
> Plans to link Sweden with mainland Europe date back to the 1800s. This dream finally became a reality with the creation of the European Union and the will to create one common economic market. The construction of the Øresund Bridge was therefore justified by economic reasons: to enhance the rapid transportation of goods and people throughout Europe in order to improve productivity and competitiveness.
>
> Although commonly called "the Øresund Bridge," the link, starting from Denmark, is actually composed of a quarter-mile-long artificial peninsula, followed by a 2.5-mile-long underwater tunnel through the artificial island of Peberholm, and finally, the nearly five-mile-long bridge. Traveling from one side of the bridge to the other with public transportation is easy, timesaving and much cheaper than traveling by car. Travel time, frequencies and costs are detailed in the following table (Øresundsbro Konsortiet 2009).
>
> | Mode of transportation | | Travel time | Frequencies | Cost |
> |---|---|---|---|---|
> | Public transit | *By train* | 35 minutes | 3/hr from 6 a.m. to 11 p.m. | $12 |
> | | | | 1/hr from 11 p.m. to 6 a.m. | |
> | | *By bus* | 40 minutes | 1/hr | $10 |
> | | | | No service on Sundays | |
> | Private car | | 45 minutes | | $50 |

in the Bo01 development was limited to 0.7 parking spaces per household in order to discourage car ownership and use. However, local residents' demand for parking exceeded that available, indicating that the scheme had ecological expectations that were more progressive than current behavior patterns. Eventually, a multistory parking garage was built in conjunction with the Turning Torso (Roberts 2008).

The parking issue was readdressed during the planning process for the neighborhood of Fullriggaren. Typically, residential neighborhoods in Malmö are required to offer 1.1 parking spaces per household. However, a new parking policy was implemented in Fullriggaren, decreasing the number of required spaces to 0.75. The policy is not a restriction on the number of parking spaces allowed to be built; it is a decrease of the number of parking spaces that are required to be built (Magnus Fahl, pers. comm.). In the end, close to the minimum number of parking spaces required were built in this neighborhood: 0.8 spaces per apartment unit. The passage of this policy is at least one step toward limiting the number of parking spaces provided in the district. Residents of Fullriggaren were surveyed in 2014, and it was found that car ownership rates were 0.6 cars per residential unit, which is less than the number of parking spaces provided. Furthermore, 61 percent of residents stated that they were satisfied with the parking situation, 14 percent were very satisfied, and only 25 percent stated that they were not satisfied (Camilla Morland, pers. comm.).

The issue of pricing parking has also been addressed in Västra Hamnen. The City of Malmö has three parking pricing zones for public, on-street parking, as outlined in Table 6.1. Like the city center, the neighborhoods of Bo01 and Flagghusen are classified as red zones, and therefore have the highest on-street parking fees in the city. The University District, Universitetsholmen, is classified as a green zone. The neighborhood of Docken, however, does not have a parking zone classification, and therefore people may park in this neighborhood for free for up to 24 hours.

Table 6.1 Parking zones for the City of Malmö

	Price per hour	Charging period
Green zone	$1.20	09:00–18:00 weekdays
White zone	$1.75	09:00–18:00 weekdays
Red zone	$2.35	09:00–20:00 weekdays
		09:00–16:00 Saturdays

Source: City of Malmö

Table 6.2 Emissions reductions from shift to carsharing vehicles in Malmö (2008)

Emissions reductions	Percentage reduction
2,530 kg CO_2	42%
1,255 g NOx	60%
15 g PM_{10}	12.5%

Source: www.civitas.eu/

Carsharing

In 2005, the City of Malmö started a program (supported by the CIVITAS Initiative) to introduce carsharing to Malmö. The program is part of the city's aim to develop a transportation system where citizens are not dependent on traditional private car ownership for all of their mobility. Membership in a carsharing organization can eliminate the need to own a private car and can reduce the number of car trips taken and vehicle miles traveled. The first Sunfleet Carsharing site was opened in 2005 close to Malmö Central Station. In 2006, the second carsharing site was established in Västra Hamnen. During 2007, two additional carsharing sites were opened in the inner city. By summer 2008, all five carsharing sites were opened, with a total of 15 cars operating in the city and over 200 members. All of Sunfleet Carsharing's cars are green vehicles, which either run on natural gas, biogas or E85 fuel (85 percent ethanol and 15 percent petroleum).

Results of the initiative were analyzed, and a survey found that those who knew about carsharing grew from 28 percent in 2003 to almost 47 percent in 2008. By virtue of the shift from petrol to green fuels, there appeared to be a reduction in emissions from the use of carsharing vehicles in Malmö. The emissions reduction estimates for 2008, based on distance traveled by participating vehicles, are detailed in Table 6.2 (CIVITAS Initiative).

A survey in 2010 found that 3 percent of Västra Hamnen residents had a carsharing membership (ITDP 2010). At that time, there were only two carsharing locations in the area. Today, there are around 18 carsharing locations in Västra Hamnen, provided by Sunfleet (Figure 6.1).

To complement the reduced parking supply in the Fullriggaren neighborhood, developers were required to provide carsharing memberships for residents for five years. Residents of the neighborhood were surveyed in 2014, and it was found that 54 percent of residents were members of a carsharing organization and an additional 12 percent planned to join.

Urban design

Over 20 architectural firms were involved in the design of Västra Hamnen. Some of the most notable architects include Swedish architect Klas Tham, architect/planner Ralph Erskine and innovative Spanish architect Santiago Calatrava. Klas Tham, in particular, was instrumental in the development and conceptual plan of the district, which includes a variety of notable design features.

6: MALMÖ: VÄSTRA HAMNEN CASE STUDY

Photo 6.7

Cafe and plaza in Västra Hamnen

Source: Photo by La Citta Vita on Flickr

STREET LAYOUT AND DESIGN

The street network of Västra Hamnen consists of a mix of individually designed streets, pedestrian ways, alleyways and open squares. Swedish architect Klas Tham himself describes the street layout as a "grid that has been distorted by the wind" (www.naturalspace.com/sweden_broadband/swedentext.htm). The district generally has a grid street network; however, within the neighborhoods, the streets are narrower and take on a more organic form. Further, the inner area of Bo01 is car-free, consisting of only pedestrian ways and bicycle paths. This structure makes it easy for cars to cross Västra Hamnen, but provides a safer environment with reduced car traffic within its various neighborhoods.

PUBLIC SPACE DESIGN

Inclusion of open green space was an important component in the design of Västra Hamnen. Several parks are located in the district such as Ankarparket and Daniaparken. The planners wanted it to be possible for citizens to walk from Västra Hamnen to the city center of Malmö through parks and green spaces. They therefore created Stapelbäddsparken, which, beyond providing a green pedestrian way, also acts as an activity center including cafes, a climbing wall, a skateboard park and an ecological playground for children. This mix has made the park a meeting place for all age groups, offering a broad range of activities promoting the health and well-being of visitors. The district also has many public plazas where people can congregate.

In a further attempt to create open public spaces, conceptual planning architect Klas Tham had the controversial idea to transform a strip of the waterfront into a promenade. This risk paid off, and today Sundspromenaden is a popular place for citizens and visitors to socialize, sunbathe and enjoy the waterfront views.

BUILDING LAYOUT AND DESIGN

The architectural firms working in Västra Hamnen were given freedom of expression to create new, innovative design structures. One outcome of this is the building layout of Bo01, designed by Klas Tham, which consists of a row of high-rise (5–7 story) flats forming a wall along the sea, creating an effective climate barrier on the southwest side of the district, with a small-scale interior including lower-rise buildings, pedestrian ways and intimate plazas. This mix gives the area a unique character.

6: MALMÖ: VÄSTRA HAMNEN CASE STUDY

Photo 6.8

Västra Hamnen waterfront

Source: Photo by La Citta Vita on Flickr

Photo 6.9

Pedestrian ways between buildings in Västra Hamnen

Source: Photo by La Citta Vita on Flickr

Table 6.3 Breakdown of residential unit size in Västra Hamnen

Studio (without kitchen)	11%
1 room	5%
2 rooms	30%
3 rooms	36%
4 rooms	13%
5+ rooms	5%

Source: City of Malmö

Photo 6.10

Residential buildings in Västra Hamnen

Source: Photo by Kristofer Steimer

Santiago Calatrava's HSB Turning Torso tower is another example of innovative design, not only its appearance, which has won international acclaim, but also due to its energy efficiency features and mix of uses.

The housing in Västra Hamnen has a mix of tenures, including tenant-owned apartments, rental apartments and private housing. This mix guarantees social diversity in the district. The size of residential units also varies, as seen in Table 6.3.

Beyond housing, Västra Hamnen contains a mix of uses, including Malmö University, the Kickum Fritid Sports Complex, the Salt & Brygga restaurant, Orkanen (Malmö's Teacher Training Department), the Malmö Business Incubator (MINC), and many other businesses, schools, restaurants and service centers. Overall, the district is home to more than 260 businesses and employs over 11,000 people (Camilla Morland, pers. comm.). The development's expansion plans include additional residential uses, as well as a focus on education, training and knowledge centers.

Mobility management

Malmö has recognized that simply building a sustainable development is not enough; ongoing effort is needed to encourage residents to adopt sustainable lifestyles. Therefore, Västra Hamnen was provided with its own mobility management office to carry out travel habit inquiries, develop informational material and work on campaigns to encourage sustainable mobility habits. A mobility management project was

> **BOX 6.3** NO RIDICULOUS CAR JOURNEYS
>
> A large number of ridiculously short car journeys (journeys shorter than three miles) are made every day in Malmö. The No Ridiculous Car Journeys campaign aims to encourage people to think about how they use their cars and to bike instead of making these short trips by car. One initiative in the campaign was a contest to win a bike by providing the details of a ridiculous car journey made in Malmö. When the campaign was launched in 2007, half of all Malmö residents were aware of it, and as a result, many have since switched their ridiculously short car trips to bike. No Ridiculous Car Journeys has gained widespread attention, both internationally and in other Swedish cities. Helsingborg, Kristianstad and Umeå have already used this campaign, and more cities are planning to do so. In Malmö, the No Ridiculous Car Journeys campaign will be repeated every spring (Malmö Stad 2009a).

carried out in Flagghusen. The project, entitled "New Address—New Travel Patterns—Flagghusen," was based on a similar project implemented by the Ardeo Centre of Excellence for the City of Malmö in 2006–2007. The Flagghusen project, conducted in November–December 2008, consisted of three steps: (1) a welcome letter was sent by mail to residents; (2) residents were contacted by phone; and (3) mobility advisors provided customized mobility advice to residents and mailed information based on the telephone conversation. The phone conversations discussed travel habits, attitudes toward different modes of travel, car ownership, how to take advantage of public transit and bicycle paths, advantages and disadvantages of different modes of transportation, and information on carsharing. Results from the previous study found that it is most effective to approach residents when they are new to a neighborhood and before they establish travel habits, in order to have a greater influence on their travel choices. The aim of the project was to provide tips and ideas on ways to simplify and improve residents' experience in the neighborhood while taking into account the environment and other residents.

Residents were given various offers, depending on their travel choices, in order to encourage them to use more sustainable modes of transportation. For example, those who mainly drove and did not own a bike were offered a free bike for a month. In addition, those not owning a car or planning to purchase a car were offered a three-month free trial membership to Sunfleet Carsharing. Respondents were also asked what type of mobility information they would be interested in receiving. The most popular item was a map of bicycle paths (69 percent), 47 percent wanted information on biking, 34 percent wanted eco-driving information, and 23 percent wanted information on carsharing. The idea is that although many residents support the idea of sustainable transportation, many need an extra push or incentive to try a more sustainable option for the first time. This first step is often the biggest hurdle to making a change in transport habits (Ardeo 2008).

Sustainable use of resources

As part of its focus on sustainable living, Västra Hamnen aimed to reduce energy use, water consumption and waste, and increase reuse and recycling. The buildings in Västra Hamnen are equipped with various energy-saving features, such as good insulation and district heating and cooling, which reduces energy use of the units. In fact, low energy use is required in Bo01, as each unit is only allowed to use 105 kwh/m^2/year. As a result, Bo01 won the European Union Commission's energy award "The Campaign for Take-Off Award" in 2000. Various studies have found that electricity and heating consumption of homes in the district is half that of an average home (Malmö Stad 2003).

The Turning Torso has also been equipped with various energy-saving features such as energy-efficient appliances, an air recirculation ventilation system and energy-saving controls for all apartments. In order to encourage reduced energy use practices, residents are offered a briefing of the environmental aspects of the building before moving in and are given information on sustainable living. Further, residents are able to check their water, heat and electricity consumption online so that they can monitor their own energy use and adjust their behavior accordingly.

6: MALMÖ: VÄSTRA HAMNEN CASE STUDY

Photo 6.11

Water channel in Västra Hamnen

Use of renewable energy sources has also been a focus in Västra Hamnen. In Bo01, the Swedish utility company Sydkraft developed a unique concept based on 100 percent locally renewable energy for the neighborhood. Energy is derived from solar power, wind power and water. 15,000 square feet of solar panels were placed on top of 10 buildings in Bo01, which produce 500 MWh for heating per year. Boel, a large wind power station located in Norra Hamnen (northern harbor), produces 6,300 MWh per year, which supplies electricity for Bo01. A further 1,300 square feet of solar cells produce electricity for apartments, heat pumps, fans and other pumps (Malmö Stad 2003).

In order to avoid runoff of rainwater into the sewage system, Västra Hamnen uses an open storm water system. Water collected in green roofs and ponds is transported in open channels to the sea. In this way, the water is biologically cleaned before reaching Öresund, and also adds to the scenery of the district.

Västra Hamnen uses a waste management system that minimizes waste, makes reuse and recycling possible, and enables use of waste and sewage as an energy source. Most apartments are equipped with a food waste disposal in the kitchen sink that grinds organic waste, which is then taken through a pipe underground to a biogas plant and transformed into biogas, which can be used as fuel in cars and buses and to produce heat and electricity. The district also has a refuse suction system. Residents separate waste into various bins. The refuse is then sucked through underground pipes to the outskirts of the area, where it is later picked up by garbage and recycling trucks, thus eliminating the need for these trucks to enter the neighborhoods.

QUANTITATIVE ANALYSIS

Västra Hamnen is located in Malmö, the third largest city in Sweden. The city has recognized the role of transportation in producing harmful emissions and has taken many steps to reduce this effect. In particular, Malmö participated in the CIVITAS SMILE initiative between 2005 and 2009, during which the city implemented several measures aimed to reduce car dependency, lower hazardous emissions from city traffic, and create a modal shift toward public transit, bicycling and carsharing.

The following analysis compares statistics from Västra Hamnen to the City of Malmö to show that even within a city as ambitious as Malmö, further reductions in carbon footprint of residents were possible due to the combination of policy and design measures present in Västra Hamnen.

Table 6.4 Statistics for Västra Hamnen and City of Malmö

	Västra Hamnen	City of Malmö
Population	7,000	313,000
Area (acres)	215*	38,500
Population density (persons/acre)	33	8
Residential units	4,000	150,000
Cars per 1,000 residents	440	480
Car parking spaces/residential unit	0.8	N/A
Residents with carsharing membership	3%	2%
Mode share for all trips		
Car	23%	41%
Public transit	17%	16%
Bicycle	31%	23%
Walking	29%	20%

* Current developed area

Source: City of Malmö, ITDP (2010)

Table 6.5 Residential unit densities in various Västra Hamnen neighborhoods

	Land area (acres)	Number of dwellings	Dwelling unit density (units/acre)
Bo01 (including Turning Torso)	54	1,450	27
Dockan	27	650	24
Flagghusen	10	630	63
Fullriggaren	11	634	58

Source: City of Malmö

Density

Västra Hamnen has a more dense settlement structure than the City of Malmö (33 persons/acre in Västra Hamnen versus 8 persons/acre in Malmö), as seen in Table 6.4. Increased density increases efficiency of resource use. The density of residential units in various neighborhoods within Västra Hamnen varies, as seen in Table 6.5. The residential unit densities in Flagghusen and Fullriggaren are particularly high, at 63 and 58 units per acre, respectively.

Car ownership rate

The car ownership rate in Malmö is higher than for other cities referenced in this book. However, Malmö is also smaller and less dense than most of the other cities discussed. The car ownership rate for Västra Hamnen is slightly lower than for the city as a whole. In Västra Hamnen, there are 440 cars per 1,000 residents, while in the City of Malmö there are 480 cars per 1,000 residents. While these rates are low compared to U.S. cities, they are high compared to large European cities, indicating that in less dense areas, although residents may travel by other modes for many daily trips, many still choose to own a car.

Mode split

Figure 6.2 compares the mode split of various trip types between Västra Hamnen residents and City of Malmö residents. The Västra Hamnen values come from an Internet-based survey of residents conducted

6: MALMÖ: VÄSTRA HAMNEN CASE STUDY

Figure 6.2

Mode split for various trip purposes for Västra Hamnen and Malmö residents

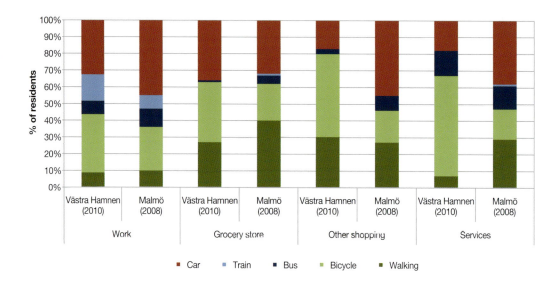

Figure 6.3

Mode split for all trips for Västra Hamnen and Malmö residents

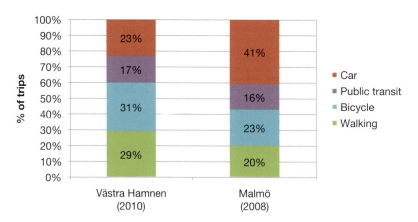

by ITDP (in collaboration with the City of Malmö) in 2010; the Malmö values are taken from the city's 2008 resident travel behavior report. The non-motorized mode share for Västra Hamnen is higher than the City of Malmö for all trip types. In Västra Hamnen, 44 percent of residents commute to work by non-motorized modes (walking or biking) versus 36 percent of Malmö residents. Furthermore, a smaller percentage of Västra Hamnen residents commute by car (33 percent versus 45 percent). Västra Hamnen's non-motorized mode share for grocery store trips is only slightly higher than Malmö's (63 percent versus 62 percent), and Västra Hamnen's mode share by car is actually higher (36 percent versus 32 percent). This demonstrates a potential to shift grocery store trips of Västra Hamnen residents to more sustainable travel modes. Västra Hamnen's non-motorized mode share for other shopping trips is much higher than for the City of Malmö (79 percent versus 46 percent), and its non-motorized mode share for service-related trips is higher as well (67 percent versus 47 percent).

Looking at overall trips taken by residents, Västra Hamnen has a more sustainable mode split than the City of Malmö, as seen in Figure 6.3. Forty-one percent of trips made by Malmö residents are by car and only 23 percent in Västra Hamnen. Further, more trips are made by bicycle (31 percent) and on foot (29 percent) in Västra Hamnen than in Malmö (23 percent and 20 percent, respectively). The share of public transit trips is similar for both.

Distance traveled

Looking at distance traveled can reveal the potential for using non-motorized travel modes. People are much more likely to walk or bike for a trip that is less than three miles than for a trip that is 15 miles or

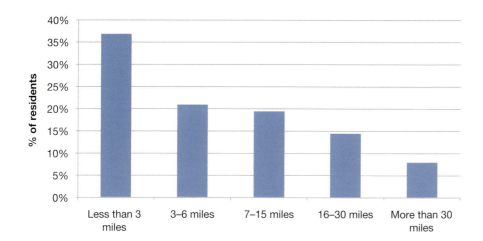

Figure 6.4

Distance to work for Västra Hamnen residents (2010)

more. According to the 2010 survey, the average distance to work for a Västra Hamnen resident is 11 miles and the average one-way commute time is 30 minutes. Figure 6.4 shows a breakdown of travel distance to work for Västra Hamnen residents. More than 35 percent of residents travel less than three miles to get to work. These short travel distances make it easier for residents to commute by walking, bicycling or public transit. Shorter travel distances also help reduce emissions generated by motorized forms of transportation. In addition, 27 percent of survey respondents stated that they work from home at least one day per week. Working from home reduces the need to travel, and thus has the potential to reduce emissions.

Residents of Västra Hamnen also do not have to travel far to get to a grocery store. One-third of residents travel less than one-third of a mile to get to a grocery store and half travel less than two-thirds of a mile. Based on survey responses, it is estimated that the average distance a resident of Västra Hamnen travels to reach a grocery store is three-quarters of a mile. This is not measuring the distance to the closest grocery store, but rather the store at which the resident chooses to shop, which may or may not be the closest store. These short distances make it easy for residents to travel to the store by foot or bicycle. Furthermore, 4 percent of survey respondents stated that they have groceries delivered at least once per month. Having groceries delivered also has the potential to reduce emissions.

LESSONS LEARNED

Today, Västra Hamnen may attract residents more so because of its attractive location near the water and city center and high-quality housing than because of its sustainable features. Therefore, while the aim was to attract residents who recognize that the high accessibility of the district makes car ownership unnecessary, many residents who did not consider the ecological focus of the district own cars and want to use them. This has caused increased demand for parking, and, as discussed, although Bo01 was initially planned as a neighborhood with limited parking, eventually a multistory parking garage was built to provide more parking. Catering to car users and making the district more car-friendly works in opposition to many of the core goals of the project.

Luckily, the City of Malmö has recognized this issue and is making more of an effort to advertise the district specifically as an eco-district, with a focus on reduced car use and ownership. In addition, a mobility management office has been developed to encourage residents to shift away from car use to more sustainable forms of transportation such as walking, biking and public transit.

New sustainable districts in other cities should keep in mind that residents are attracted by a variety of features, not just environmental ones. Therefore, it is important to market the focus on sustainable living and reduced car ownership from the beginning and also to provide an ongoing effort (such as a mobility management office) to encourage sustainable transportation habits.

Our next case study, like Västra Hamnen, was created to be a signature development, and features distinctive, contemporary architecture. However, unlike Västra Hamnen, Greenwich Millennium Village, in London, is a more challenging location, less centrally located and with fewer destination sites within a short bike ride.

REFERENCES
Ardeo (2008) *Ny adress—nya resvanor Inflyttade i Flagghusen Gatukontoret*, Malmö: Ardeo.
Communication with Camilla Morland, Streets and Parks Department, City of Malmö, June 2015.
Communication with Csaba Gyarmati, Transportation and Highways Department, City of Malmö, August 2010.
Communication with Magnus Fahl, Streets and Parks Department, City of Malmö, July 2015.
ITDP (2010) Internet-based survey of Västra Hamnen residents, conducted in collaboration with the City of Malmö
Malmö Stad (2003) *Västra Hamnen—the Bo01 Area: A City for People and the Environment*, Malmö: Malmö Stad.
Malmö Stad (2008) *Malmöbornas resvanor och attityder till trafik och miljö 2008*, Malmö: Malmö Stad.
Malmö Stad (2009a) *Guide Western Harbor*, Malmö: Malmö Stad.
Malmö Stad (2009b) *Improving Malmö's Traffic Environment*, Malmö: Malmö Stad.
Malmö Stad (2010) *The Western Harbour Facts and Figures 2010*, Malmö: Malmö Stad.
Malmö Stad (2015) *Västra Hamnen: Current Urban Development*, Malmö: Malmö Stad.
Malmö Stad: http://malmo.se/vastrahamnen.
Øresundsbro Konsortiet (2009) *Øresundsbron Annual Report*, Copenhagen and Malmö: Øresundsbro Konsortiet.
Roberts, H. (2008) *Urban Design Best Practice Case Study—Bo01, Malmö, Sweden. Bo01 City of Tomorrow*, Malmö.
Sunfleet: www.sunfleet.com/bilpooler/malmo/vastra-hamnen/.

7
London
Greenwich Millennium Village case study

BACKGROUND

Greenwich Millennium Village (GMV) was selected as a best practice case study because it is an excellent example of a mixed-use, brownfield redevelopment project situated in a location well served by transit with limited through-car traffic and strict parking restrictions. While car ownership rates in the development are only marginally better than in the surrounding area, car use is significantly lower. This is especially noteworthy given the challenging location, distance from major activity centers and geographic isolation caused by the River Thames, limiting bike connectivity, resulting in residents being more dependent on public transit.

GMV is located on the Greenwich Peninsula, a 300-acre brownfield redevelopment site formerly occupied by the town gasworks, on the southern banks of the River Thames in southeast London, about five miles from London city center. In 1997, English Partnerships[1] (the English regeneration agency)

Figure 7.1

Map of Greenwich Millennium Village

Source: Map by Amy Smith

109

7: LONDON: GMV CASE STUDY

Photo 7.1

Greenwich Millennium Village

Source: Photo by Andrew Sparkes (www.pinholedesign.co.uk)

> **BOX 7.1**
> **GMV SITE FACTS**
>
> *Developer:*
> Greenwich Millennium Village Limited (GMVL)
>
> *Architect:*
> Ralph Erskine
>
> *Population:*
> 2,300
>
> *Projected population:*
> 5,800
>
> *Developed area:*
> 50 acres
>
> *Total area:*
> 72 acres
>
> *Current density:*
> 46 persons/acre
>
> *Projected density:*
> 81 persons/acre
>
> *Current residential units:*
> 1,095
>
> *Planned residential units:*
> 2,840
>
> *Construction began:*
> 1999
>
> *Planned completion:*
> 2035
>
> *Distance from city center:*
> 5 miles
>
> *Cars:*
> 350 cars/1,000 residents
>
> *Parking spaces/residence:*
> 0.7
>
> *Non-motorized mode share:*
> 32%
>
> *Public transit mode share:*
> 49%

took the commitment to transform the peninsula, one of the largest development sites in London, into a new residential community. The regeneration project is currently in phase 2 of a 20-year build program, which will see 10,000 residential units, leisure and retail facilities, as well as educational and health centers. GMV covers just 72 acres on the southeastern side of the Greenwich Peninsula.

The project was the first Millennium Community to be identified by English Partnerships and is being developed by Greenwich Millennium Village Limited, a joint venture between Countryside Properties and Taylor Wimpey. The Millennium Communities Program was launched by English Partnerships alongside the Department for Communities and Local Government to create seven exemplar sustainable communities nationwide. Each of the seven communities were to incorporate high-density housing, green spaces, good transportation links and easy access to shops and recreation facilities, producing quality places where people want to live. In order to ensure that sustainability goals are met, the Millennium Communities Program has set standards for energy efficiency, water consumption, transportation, building materials, recycling and health and safety on-site. In line with these goals, the housing at GMV is of modern, environmentally friendly design, and the development aims to cut primary energy use by 80 percent, compared to traditional developments of similar size, using low-energy building techniques and renewable energy technologies. The project aims to reduce car dependency through giving priority to bicyclists and pedestrians, providing good access to public transportation, and restricting

> **BOX 7.2** LONDON CONGESTION CHARGE
>
> The London congestion charge is a fee for motorists traveling within the congestion charge zone of London. The purpose of the fee is to reduce congestion and raise funds for improving London's transportation system. The congestion charge was initially introduced in Central London in 2003. The congestion zone was then extended to parts of West London in 2007. Currently, vehicles are charged $18 per day for entering the congestion zone. A fine is applied to those who do not pay the charge. Violations are monitored through the use of automatic number plate recognition cameras. Transport for London, the city's public transportation agency, administers the charge. Money collected is invested to enhance bus and underground service in order to take over some of the demand shifted from cars. Immediate effects of the charge included less traffic congestion, faster travel times, more public transit users and reduced emissions (Transport for London 2008). However, studies have shown that these results appear to be decreasing over time.

and pricing car parking. The natural environment is also a focus, and GMV includes an ecology park, bicycle paths and recreational areas.

It is not surprising that the first community in this program was selected to be located in London, one of the largest and most congested cities in Europe, with a high demand for more housing. London politicians and citizens alike have long recognized the need to reduce car use in the city and have taken various actions, such as the implementation of a congestion charge in central London in 2003 (see Box 7.2). The charge was successful in reducing congestion in Inner London; however, car use remains prevalent in Outer London. Therefore, it is important for developments such as GMV, located outside the city center, to implement strategies aimed at reducing car dependency.

GMV is marketed as an experiment in sustainable development. New residents are given a packet of information on sustainable living when they move in. Various studies have shown that residents support the concept and ethos of the village. Further, they appreciate the sustainable design features and enjoy being part of the special community, demonstrating the project's success not only as a sustainable development, but as a livable community as well (Cherry and Hodkinson 2009).

To date, 1,095 homes, a primary school, a health center, an ecology park and a village square with shops have been completed, covering a development area of 50 acres (see Figure 7.1). All of the residential units are currently occupied. The homes completed include a number of live/work units and a wide range of affordable housing. Phases 3, 4 and 5 are currently under construction, including additional housing, retail and office space, with a total proposed developed area of 72 acres for the entire village.

PLANNING PROCESS

In 1997, English Partnerships launched a competition to design and build Greenwich Millennium Village, the first community in the Millennium Communities Program. The competition was won by Greenwich Millennium Village Limited (GMVL), a joint venture between Countryside Properties and Taylor Wimpey. English Partnerships and GMVL signed a Section 106 agreement (see Box 7.3) in which GMVL agreed to build a sustainable mixed-use residential development of 1,400 dwellings with 20 percent designated as affordable housing. For the affordable housing portion of the development, GMVL is working in association with social housing partners Moat Housing. GMVL also agreed to contribute a specified sum for bus improvements in the area and to submit a parking garage management plan.

In return, English Partnerships agreed to fund the Millennium Busway, a bus-only lane running through the development, as well as a state-of-the-art integrated school and health center, which opened in 2001. English Partnerships also agreed to produce an annual travel monitoring study including analysis of mode split and parking demand of GMV residents in addition to a strategy plan for reducing car use. An annual travel survey of residents was conducted up until 2005, but was then unfortunately

7: LONDON: GMV CASE STUDY

Photo 7.2

Live/work units in GMV

Source: Photo by Frederique Siegel

> **BOX 7.3 SECTION 106 AGREEMENTS**
> These agreements refer to Section 106 of the British Parliament's Town and Country Planning Act of 1990, which regulates the development of land in England and Wales. Section 106 permits local authorities and developers to make agreements over the use of land, including planning obligations by the developer to contribute toward sustainable communities and offset the costs of the external effects of the development. Contributions by the developer may include cash, infrastructure investments or provision of services. Examples include provision of new schools, public space, affordable housing, new roads and public transit. Section 106 agreements are legally binding and are linked to the granting of planning permission. Each agreement is different and depends on the unique needs of each community. Some agreements may include measures aimed at reducing transport-related emissions. Transport-related measures that have been included by the Greenwich Council (specifically for the Woolwich Town Centre Development) include: provision of carsharing, controls on parking permits, emission-related parking charges, provision of electric vehicle charging points and use of biofuel in delivery vehicles (Birch 2010).

Photo 7.3

Millennium Primary School in GMV

Source: Photo by ©Paul Eccleston Arthouse Ltd

discontinued. Ongoing monitoring studies are important to ensure that developments are continuing to meet the goals set for them.

Construction of GMV began in 1999, and the first homes were occupied by 2000. Phases 1 and 2 of the building process were completed by 2002, producing 1,095 residential units, a village square with shops, an artificial lake and an ecology park.

In 2006, a new Section 106 agreement was signed between the Greenwich Peninsula landowners, English Partnerships, and GMVL. This agreement increased the planned development size from 1,400 to 2,900 residential units and increased the required share of affordable housing from 20 percent to 35 percent. The agreement laid out the plans for phases 3, 4 and 5 of the development, which would include construction of around 1,800 additional new homes, 15,000 square feet of retail spaces, 70,000 square feet of work space, a community center and a nursery. The initial planned completion date for phases 3, 4 and 5 was 2014 (www.englishpartnerships.co.uk/gmv.htm).

However, due to the subsequent economic recession and changing priorities revolving around planning for the 2012 Olympic Games in London, progress on the development was delayed. A revised plan was approved in 2012, and a new Section 106 agreement was signed between GMVL, the Homes and Communities Agency, and the Royal Borough of Greenwich. The plan represents the final stages of the comprehensive redevelopment of this key site, which is important to the successful regeneration of the Greenwich Peninsula. The revised plan similarly outlines development of a mixed-use, mixed-income development, including residential, retail, office and institutional uses. The residential portion calls for construction of 1,746 dwelling units beyond the initial 1,095 that were built as part of phases 1 and 2. This is slightly fewer than the number of dwelling units proposed in the 2006 agreement. Unfortunately, under the revised agreement, the proportion of affordable housing was reduced from 35 percent back to 20 percent, due to concerns that higher provision of affordable units would make the development financially unviable. The revised plan calls for provision of 0.45 car parking spaces per residential unit, 1.3 bike parking spaces per unit, and Section 106 contributions for bus capacity enhancements and waterfront transit enhancements. Construction is currently underway, and is planned to be complete by 2035 (Moireira and Brown 2012).

7: LONDON: GMV CASE STUDY

Photo 7.4

View of GMV and O2 Arena from water

Source: Photo by Andrew Sparkes www.pinholedesign.co.uk

KEY POLICY AND DESIGN MEASURES

The Millennium Communities Program recognized reduced car dependency as a key sustainability issue. This is especially apparent in the City of London, which has limited room for additional parking spaces and a high level of traffic congestion. Spurred by these concerns, GMV has incorporated several policy and design measures aimed at reducing car dependency and promoting other, more sustainable forms of transportation.

Parking

As part of its strategy to reduce car dependency, parking at GMV is restricted and generally located away from individual properties. Two floors of parking garage are located beneath two of the apartment buildings built during phase 1. In phase 2, car parking facilities were separated from apartment units and located at the edge of the development. Overall, there are 884 parking spaces currently provided as part of phases 1 and 2 of the development. Approximately 770 of these spaces are for residents, for a ratio of 0.7 spaces per residential unit. Proposed parking provision for phases 3, 4 and 5 of the development is even stricter. A total of 881 parking spaces are proposed for the new development, and, of these, 779 spaces are designated for residents, providing a parking ratio for phases 3, 4 and 5 of 0.45 spaces per residential unit. This proposed level of parking provision was determined based on surveys of existing parking occupancy in the existing development. Transport for London (TfL), which reviewed the plan, supports this reduction in parking provision as being in line with the London Plan standards. The proposed parking plan for the new development also includes disabled parking, spaces for carsharing vehicles and electric vehicle charging stations. As part of the approval process, TfL also recommended conducting ongoing monitoring of parking to be included in the travel plan as part of the Section 106 agreement for the development (Moireira and Brown 2012).

In line with parking management best practices, parking spaces at GMV are unbundled from apartment units, so residents who choose to have a parking space must pay for it separately from their residence. Residents don't pay for a specific parking space, but rather for a "right to park," which means they can enter the parking garage and must then search for an available space. The price per space has

7: LONDON: GMV CASE STUDY

Photo 7.5

North Greenwich station designed by Will Alsop

continued to increase since the development was first built, and was approximately $30,000 per parking space in 2010 (Marcello Burbante, pers. comm.).

Only residents who have purchased a space are allowed to park in the residential parking garages; visitors are not allowed. Visitors are expected either to park temporarily in the bays on the main roads, which are frequently ticketed by the council, or in the public parking lot next to the North Greenwich transit station located a half-mile northwest of GMV. However, during school holidays, people are informally allowed to park in the school's parking lot. In addition, residents often rent out their spaces to neighbors during the winter holidays by advertising on bulletin boards in the shared spaces. In this way, residents have taken it upon themselves to manage the existing parking supply as efficiently as possible, treating it as a valuable commodity.

Public transportation

Good public transportation access is essential given the low provision of parking on-site. GMV residents have several public transit options available; the most highly used is the London Underground. The Jubilee Line of the Underground was extended to Stratford in 1999, including the North Greenwich station, located a half-mile northwest of GMV. This high-capacity station was designed by Will Alsop of Alsop and Störmer and can handle more than 22,000 passengers per hour (http://gmv.gb.com/). From here, residents can access Central London in less than 25 minutes by Underground and are one stop away from a major office development at Canary Wharf. Directly above the underground station is a major new bus terminal designed by Sir Norman Foster, which handles eight routes and 56 buses per hour during peak hours (Kim Smith, pers. comm.). The station area has an emphasis on walking, biking and the use of public transit over the car. A two-lane dedicated busway, called the Millennium Busway, runs from the station through GMV, with two stops located within the village. In addition, within walking distance of GMV, to the east of the North Greenwich transit station on the Thames, is the North Greenwich Pier, which offers commuter boat service to other parts of London, both east and west.

7: LONDON: GMV CASE STUDY

Photo 7.6

Millennium Busway in GMV

The transit pricing system within the City of London is fairly complicated and includes zone-based, time-based, quality-based and market-based pricing. Users pay based on the number of zones they travel between. Additionally, users pay more to travel during the peak or "rush-hour" periods of the day. The pricing is also quality-based in that different modes of travel have different fare levels. For example, fares are lower for buses than for the Underground. Market-based pricing refers to the availability of various unlimited travel passes, ranging from one-day passes to annual passes. In order to simplify the process of calculating the appropriate fare, Transport for London offers a contactless smartcard called an Oyster Card, which must be validated when entering and exiting the transit system (see Box 7.4). The cards can be loaded with single tickets, period tickets or travel permits. Since fares vary so much, a system is in place that will cap the price for certain types of travel (www.tfl.gov.uk/).

> **BOX 7.4 OYSTER CARD**
> Transport for London offers an integrated smartcard, the Oyster Card, which can be used on all public transportation within the city. It can be loaded with electronic cash for pay-as-you-go travel and/or period passes. There is an option to add funds automatically once the balance falls below a user-defined threshold, eliminating the need for users to have to remember to refill their cards. Moreover, fares paid using the card are significantly lower than those paid by cash, providing a further incentive for regular users to obtain an Oyster Card. Card use is beneficial for the transportation system as well, particularly on buses, because it reduces the boarding time of passengers compared with paying a cash fare to the driver, increasing average speeds. Therefore, provision of the Oyster Card improves quality of service for transit users. Furthermore, Transport for London can use travel pattern data collected through the cards when deciding service changes such as adding new routes and targeted capacity expansion (www.tfl.gov.uk/).

7: LONDON: GMV CASE STUDY

Photo 7.7

Green space behind residential units in GMV

Source: Photo ©Paul Eccleston Arthouse Ltd

Bicycle and pedestrian infrastructure

GMV strives to promote bicycling and walking. Within GMV, secure bicycle storage facilities are provided for every housing unit, and two or three bicycle parking spaces are available per unit, including several covered, weather-protective bicycle parking facilities. A network of bicycle and pedestrian routes runs throughout the village and beyond, connecting the development to the surrounding areas along the Greenwich Peninsula. For example, a pedestrian walkway leads from GMV to the O2 Arena, a large sports and music venue located in the Millennium Dome on the northern side of the peninsula, which was used during the 2012 Olympics. However, direct bike connections are not available across the River Thames. In order to cross the river with a bike, riders must take a ferry, reducing the fluidity of travel.

Phases 3, 4 and 5 of the development will similarly provide high-quality bicycle and pedestrian paths, improving links and crossings to existing facilities and transit stations, and prioritizing direct access by walking and biking over driving. The new development will also provide secure, covered bicycle parking for residents, visitors, retail and offices (Moireira and Brown 2012).

Carsharing

Two carsharing vehicles, provided by Zipcar, are located just to the north of GMV. In addition, two Zipcar carsharing vehicles are located in a parking lot off of Tunnel Avenue, about a quarter-mile south of GMV. Other than these four vehicles, no other carsharing vehicles are located on Greenwich Peninsula. There seems to be a potential to locate more carsharing vehicles on this site, particularly inside the GMV parking garages themselves. The plan for GMV phases 3, 4 and 5 calls for carsharing vehicles to be located in the new parking facilities.

Urban design

GMV was designed by masterplanning architect Ralph Erskine to be a modern urban village, incorporating high-density residential units with green public spaces and providing opportunities for leisure activities

7: LONDON: GMV CASE STUDY

Photo 7.8
Lake and ecology park in GMV
Source: Photo ©Paul Eccleston Arthouse Ltd

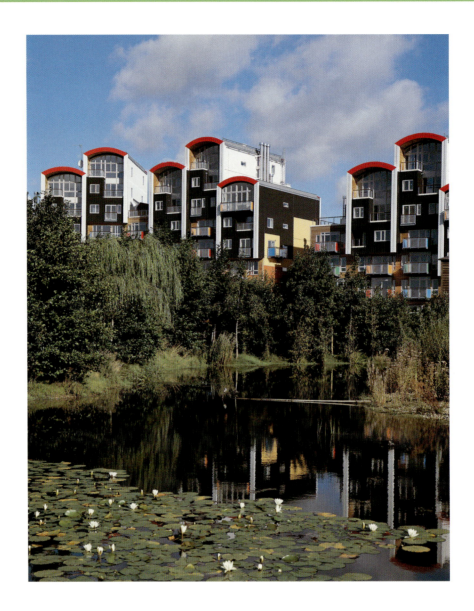

and shopping. Erskine was known for his preference for design with limited through-car traffic. He also worked on the Bo01 car-free development in Malmö. In line with these principles, Erskine's vision for GMV was to create a community where the pedestrian has priority over the car.

STREET LAYOUT AND DESIGN
Main thoroughfares run along the northwest and southwest borders of the development. Further, two main thoroughfares run through GMV. West Parkside bisects the development, while Southern Way splits off from West Parkside midway through the development and runs southward. A two-lane dedicated busway that starts at North Greenwich station passes through the village along West Parkside, turning onto Southern Way (Figure 7.1). The busway, distinguished by its brick-red color, is separated from car lanes by a green median. On the south side of the village is a road that leads to the school parking lot. Other than these roads, the development is car-free and priority is given to bicyclists and pedestrians.

PUBLIC SPACE DESIGN
Provision of public spaces was an important component of the design. The village includes an ecology park, a village square and landscaped courtyards. The ecology park, covering 50 acres, includes two

7: LONDON: GMV CASE STUDY

Photo 7.9

Landscaped courtyard in GMV

Source: Photo ©Paul Eccleston Arthouse Ltd

Photo 7.10

Colorful plaza in GMV

Source: Photo ©Paul Eccleston Arthouse Ltd

lakes and a thriving wildlife population. In addition, garden squares are located throughout the residential areas. The design gives priority to the bicyclist and pedestrian, providing pedestrian and bicycle pathways separated from motor vehicle traffic throughout the village. Furthermore, safety is enhanced through monitoring of transit stops, bicycle routes and pedestrian areas by CCTV.

LAND USE PLANNING AND DESIGN

GMV was designed from the beginning as a mixed-use development combining residences, retail, commercial and leisure spaces. Phase 1 of the development consists of blocks of flats 8–10 stories high, surrounding inner courtyards, with two floors of parking garages beneath. The highest buildings are located on the northern side of the development, along the River Thames, to provide more waterfront views. Phase 2 includes a mix of lower-rise flats up to six stories and terraced houses situated around public squares with car parking in a separate block at the side of the development. The residential units include a mix of tenure types.

The village square is located near the center of the development, conveniently located within walking distance of residential units so that residents can easily conduct shopping trips and errands by bike or on foot. The uses in the village square include a small grocery store, a pharmacy and several cafes. Overall, the development includes nearly 50,000 square feet of commercial space along with community facilities such as a school and health center (www.countryside-properties-corporate.com).

Sustainable use of resources

The Millennium Communities Program has set several sustainability standards regarding energy efficiency and water consumption. In order to comply with these standards, GMV homes were designed to minimize energy and water use. Energy-saving features include good insulation, design incorporating use of daylighting and natural ventilation, and community heating provided through a combined heat and power (CHP) system. Further, electricity generated during the operation of the CHP is used for powering lighting in parking garages and other public areas, and the surplus energy is sold back to the grid. These features combined were found to reduce CO_2 produced from energy use by 67 percent compared to a benchmark all-electric system. Owing to its focus on sustainability, GMV was awarded an EcoHomes "Excellent" rating in August 2001.

Water-conserving features in the residential units include efficient taps and low-flow showers. In addition, a water harvesting system on a landscaped roof of one of the parking garages provides water for landscaping irrigation. Through application of these features, water consumption at GMV was reduced by 35 percent compared to the 1999-based benchmark value (Cherry and Hodkinson 2009).

QUANTITATIVE ANALYSIS

Analysis of statistics for GMV compared to other parts of London demonstrates the effect of the various policy and design measures applied in the development. GMV has a much higher residential density than the Greenwich District, in which it is located, or London as a whole. Furthermore, a much smaller proportion of the trips made by GMV residents (18 percent) are by car than for Greenwich (44 percent) or London (42 percent). The car ownership rate per resident is lower for GMV than for London (see Table 7.1).

Table 7.1 Statistics for GMV, Greenwich and London

	GMV	Greenwich	London
Population	2,300	223,000	8,600,000
Area (acres)	50*	11,600	420,000
Population density (persons/acre)	46	19	20
Residential units	1,095	100,000	3,000,000
Cars per 1,000 residents	350	350	370
Car parking spaces/residential unit	0.70	N/A	N/A
Mode share for all trips			
Car	18%	44%	42%
Public transit	49%	29%	25%
Bicycle	4%	1%	2%
Walking	29%	26%	31%

* Current developed area

Sources: Rutherfords (2005), Transport for London (2009), Greater London Authority

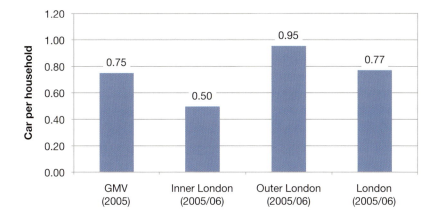

Figure 7.2

Cars per household in GMV and London

Car ownership rates

Figure 7.2 provides a comparison of car ownership rate per household for various segments of London. The rate for GMV falls between that of Inner London, where households are generally less car-dependent, and that of Outer London, where households are typically more car-dependent. The rate for GMV also falls below that for London. These figures demonstrate that many households in GMV choose to live car-free, although the car ownership rate is still not quite as low as it is in Inner London.

Mode split

However, while car ownership in GMV is higher than for Inner London, car use in GMV appears to be much lower than for other areas of London, even Inner London. As seen in Figure 7.3, only 18 percent of trips made by GMV residents are by car, which is much lower than for Greenwich (44 percent), Inner London (29 percent), Outer London (51 percent) and London (43 percent). The GMV data were collected through a survey of residents conducted to fulfill the requirements for the Section 106 agreement, and included in the Travel Monitoring Study 2005 Report. Unfortunately, 2005 was the last year this survey was conducted, so more recent data were not available.

Public transit use is high in GMV, particularly for trips to work. Indeed, the majority of GMV commuters (79 percent) travel to work by public transit. The breakdown by type of public transit shows that 73 percent of commuters travel to work by London Underground. This is not surprising given GMV's

7: LONDON: GMV CASE STUDY

Figure 7.3

Mode split for all trips in GMV, Greenwich and London

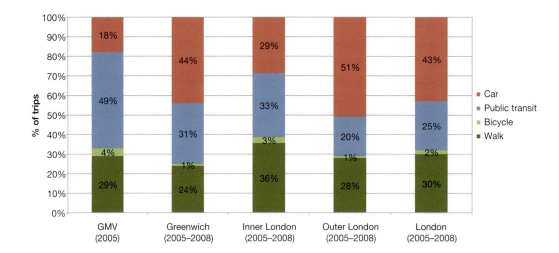

Figure 7.4

Mode of travel to work for GMV residents (2005)

easy access to the Jubilee Line, connecting the development to Central London, and the high cost of driving to central London due to the city's congestion charge. Figure 7.4 shows that a much larger proportion of GMV residents (79 percent) commute to work by public transit than Inner London residents (59 percent), Outer London residents (38 percent) and overall London residents (46 percent). Further, the proportion of GMV residents commuting to work by car is very low.

Although a small proportion of GMV residents walk or bike to work, a much higher number walk or bike for other trip purposes such as traveling to school and shopping (see Figure 7.5). Nearly one-third of those who study walk to school; however, almost a quarter drive. These results are likely due to the mix of student types; children are more likely to walk or bike to school within the village while adults taking classes outside the district might be more likely to drive.

Furthermore, while about half of the residents use their car for their main weekly food shopping trip, one-third walk or bike for this trip. Many may travel to Sainsbury's for this trip, the first low-energy food store in Britain, which is located just south of GMV (within a half-mile of most residences). The store is 50 percent more efficient than a standard supermarket, incorporating use of natural light, high levels of insulation, passive ventilation and underfloor heating systems (http://gmv.gb.com/). However, while the supermarket has a focus on energy sustainability, it seems to have overlooked transportation sustainability as it caters to the car; the store is located next to an extensive parking lot with more than 300 free-to-use spaces. The ease of accessible parking might encourage GMV residents to drive to the store rather than bike or walk. The store is also accessible by bus; however, Figure 7.5 shows that few residents travel by bus to the grocery store. Not included in Figure 7.5 are those who have groceries delivered. The resident survey found that 8 percent have groceries delivered to their residence

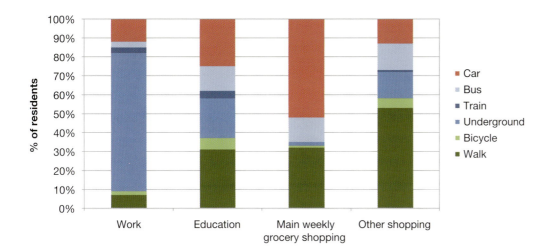

Figure 7.5

GMV resident mode of travel for various trip types (2005)

(Rutherfords 2005). This reduces the number of trips made by residents, but the effect on carbon footprint of these trips depends on delivery vehicle fuel and scheduling efficiency.

In addition, more than half of residents walk or bike for other shopping trips. Providing a wide variety of shops in the village makes it more convenient for residents to walk for these trips. The survey of residents was taken in 2005, and the number of shops in the village square has been expanded since that time, so it is likely that a more current survey would show a higher proportion of walking and biking trips.

Many live/work units are provided at GMV to encourage residents to work from home, thus reducing the number of commute trips. Several more live/work units are planned as part of phases 3, 4 and 5. Overall, it was found that 7 percent of GMV residents work from home. This is similar to the proportion for Greenwich (7 percent) and slightly lower than for Inner London (9 percent), Outer London (9 percent) and London (9 percent) (Rutherfords 2005).

The results of this analysis show that the policy and design measures applied in GMV appear to have had a strong influence on reducing car trips made by residents; however, potential remains to increase bicycle trips, particularly within the development.

LESSONS LEARNED

Given the location of GMV, including its distance from London city center, and lack of direct bike connections to Central London, it is not realistic to expect most commuters to travel to work by bicycle or on foot. GMV's focus on providing good public transit access, combined with the existence of London's congestion fee, have resulted in an impressive commute mode share of 79 percent by public transit. Like San Francisco, London experiences very high transit ridership, but the transit is at capacity. Bicycling is seen as a desirable relief. In GMV, there is limited opportunity for a shift toward more bicycling unless bicycle connectivity is improved, such as providing a bicycle facility crossing of the River Thames. This could increase the proportion of residents commuting to work by bike and help to reduce demand on the public transit system.

In addition, room for improvement lies in travel choices of residents within the GMV development. About half of residents travel by car for their weekly grocery shopping trip. An increase in the number and diversity of stores located at GMV could encourage more walking and bicycle trips within the development as opposed to driving. This finding also suggests an increased market for grocery home deliveries. Eight percent of residents already have groceries delivered. Further marketing of this option could encourage more residents to use a delivery service. However, it is important to ensure that these deliveries are made using sustainable transportation practices. By chaining deliveries to several residents, the number of overall trips could be reduced. Furthermore, making deliveries by bicycle rather than motorized vehicle would cut transportation emissions. Sihlcity, a retail and leisure development in Zurich that heavily restricts parking, has successfully implemented a bicycle-based delivery service. Such a service could be piloted in GMV and should be included in similar development projects.

Provision of live/work units is a beneficial feature at GMV, allowing residents to work from home. At the time of the survey in 2005, the presence of these units did not seem to increase the proportion of residents working from home above that of the surrounding area; however, promotion of these units and addition of units in phases 3, 4 and 5 should encourage more residents to work from home. Home offices have the obvious benefit of reducing commute trips. However, some studies have shown an increase in other trips due to the increased flexibility of the work schedule. This is another reason why it is essential to provide amenities within walking distance of residences in order to encourage residents to walk and bike for their daily needs rather than traveling outside the development by car to access goods and services.

The previous three masterplanned developments have shown that there is exceptional promise for car-lite development on former port and industrial lands, which are often proximate to urban cores. Cities such as Oakland, San Diego, New Orleans, Pittsburg, Philadelphia and Baltimore, where the port or waterfront areas are in transition, have potential for similar redevelopment and revitalization.

The next case study is also a masterplanned development, however on a greenfield site. While all of the previous case studies have focused on urban infill redevelopment, the last study provides a unique example of a suburban masterplanned community, with a focus on reducing car trips for inner city travel.

NOTE

1   English Partnerships was a non-departmental public body funded through the Department for Communities and Local Government (2004). It was responsible for land acquisition and assembly and major development projects, alone or in joint partnership with private sector developers. In December 2008, its powers passed to a successor body, the new Homes and Communities Agency.

REFERENCES

Birch, C. (2010) *Using Section 106 Agreements to Improve Air Quality*, London: Communities and Local Government.
Cherry, A. and Hodkinson, R. (2009) "Millennium homes revisited," *Ingenia*, 41, December 2009, available at: www.ingenia.org.uk/ingenia/issues/issue41/Cherry_Hodkinson.pdf (accessed July 2015).
Communication with Kim Smith, Transportation Planning and Strategy Manager, Greenwich Council, May 2010.
Communication with Marcello Burbante, Greenwich Millennium Village Ltd (GMVL), September 2010.
Department for Communities and Local Government (2004) *Contributing to Sustainable Communities: An Approach to Planning Obligations*, London: Eland House.
English Partnerships (2007) *Millennium Communities Programme*, London: English Partnerships.
Moireira, S. and Brown, F. (2012) *Greenwich Millennium Village Phases 3, 4 and 5 Final Report*, Ref. 12/0022/O.
Rutherfords—Highway & Transport Planning (2005) *Greenwich Millennium Village: Travel Monitoring Study, 2005 Report*, Cambridge: Rutherfords.
Transport for London (2008) *Central London Congestion Charging: Impacts Monitoring—Sixth Annual Report*, London: Transport for London.
Transport for London (2009) *Travel in London: Key Trends and Developments Report Number 1*, London: Transport for London.
Transport for London (2010) *Travel in London: Report 2*, London: Transport for London.

8

The Randstad

Houten case study

BACKGROUND

Students of urban planning know from history that in the early nineteenth century, London was at the forefront of new town planning, a scheme designed to de-concentrate the crowded industrial city but in a rational, orderly manner. That planning tradition inspired the Netherlands after World War II, whereby Dutch urban policy included very intentional, compact satellite cities on high-frequency rail corridors, like "pearls on a string." The Randstadt in the Netherlands metropolitan core includes Amsterdam, Rotterdam and Utrecht, all traditional urban centers. Houten is among a collection of satellite new towns meant to de-concentrate the traditional centers while avoiding the worst of sprawl. Among the Dutch new towns, Houten stands out for its intentional (by design) privileging of the bicycle and its internal circulation. The bike system is complemented by fast convenient access to Utrecht and Amsterdam by train; however, as we will see, the dispersed nature of the Randstadt's employment centers means that Houten exhibits higher car ownership rates than those found in the other case study sites, although the rates are still impressive compared to other suburban locations.

Houten, a city in the province of Utrecht in the Netherlands, is a unique example of an entire city designed and built to prioritize bicyclists, pedestrians and transit. It is a greenfield development with excellent regional transit access, high-quality bicycle infrastructure, provision of public bikes and carsharing, and application of employer contributions and educational programs to promote bicycling. Non-motorized transportation use is higher in Houten than in comparable cities while car use is lower.

The city's innovative traffic layout was developed in 1968 and approved by the city council, though it differed radically from the norm of car-oriented planning. The key focus of the design was to limit intra-city car use and give priority to traffic safety for pedestrians and bicyclists. Core design measures include features to slow car traffic such as narrow roads and frequent turns, and separation of bicycle paths from car traffic whenever possible.

The basic layout of the city consists of two train stations, each surrounded by a ring road with a radius of approximately one half mile, connected to form a figure eight. The rest of the city is covered by an extensive, 80-mile network of shared-use paths with low traffic speeds by design. There are 31 residential districts, each of which is only accessible to cars via the peripheral ring roads encircling the town. However, the network of routes for bicyclists and pedestrians includes more direct connection points between neighborhoods and a thoroughfare that passes directly through the town center, providing filtered permeability for bicyclists and pedestrians. The majority of schools and important buildings are located along this thoroughfare. Due to this design, bicycling is the most direct mode of transportation and is often even faster than travel by car.[1]

Houten's innovative design features, along with the city's persistent policies to favor bicyclists and pedestrians, have resulted in numerous measured benefits, including improved bicyclist and pedestrian safety, increased activity levels of residents, and reduced use of motorized vehicles. Furthermore, this case study demonstrates that innovative design features are not limited to new districts within a city, but can be applied to new cities as a whole.

BOX 8.1
CITY OF HOUTEN SITE FACTS

Architect:
Rob Derks

Population:
48,000

Urban area:
2,030 acres

Urban density:
24 persons/acre

Number of residential units:
18,400

Distance from Utrecht city center:
5 miles

Cars:
415 cars/1,000 residents

Parking spaces/residence:
1.1

Non-motorized mode share:
55%

Public transport mode share:
11%

Households with a carsharing membership:
2%

8: THE RANDSTAD: HOUTEN CASE STUDY

Figure 8.1

Map of Houten

Source: Map by Amy Smith

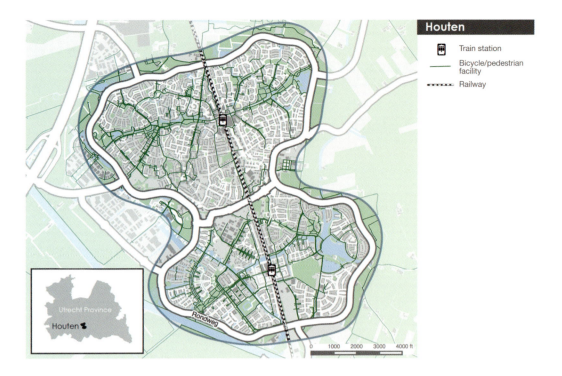

PLANNING PROCESS

In 1966, the national government identified Houten, then a small village with a population of about 3,000, as a high growth area and mandated a growth plan be developed to accommodate an eventual population of 100,000. Locals balked at the extreme expectations for growth and ultimately compromised on providing a plan for an eventual population of 25,000. In 1968, Dutch architect Rob Derks offered a plan heavily focused on filtered permeability: a dense network of direct routes for bicyclists and a course network of general roads, offering limited city center access to cars (see Box 8.2). The city council, which was then made up of civilians and farmers and no politicians, approved Derk's plan, which they believed would provide a more livable quality to their city. They hired four city advisors (including Rob Derks) with expertise in architecture, city planning and transportation engineering to implement the plan. This combination of technical and planning expertise was key to the success of the development.

In 1974, an agreement was made with the national government to fund the first ring road. Construction began in 1978. The ring road encircling the City of Houten, with a population of around 25,000, was completed by the late 1980s. Further infrastructure was publicly funded, both through the local government and using grants from the regional and national governments.

BOX 8.2 FILTERED PERMEABILITY

Filtered permeability is the concept that networks should be designed in a way that favors pedestrians and bicyclists, making travel by these modes more direct, more convenient and even faster than traveling by car. This approach may even include strategies to limit or restrict movement by cars. The goal is to encourage walking and bicycling and, as a result, reduce emissions. Filtered permeability applications often include separating pedestrian and bicycling paths from roads for motorized vehicles. Houten has applied many principles of filtered permeability including providing a limited network for motorized vehicles while providing a more extensive network for pedestrians and bicyclists. As a result, traveling by bike is often more direct and even faster than traveling by car. In addition, segregated bicycle crossings have been built at critical locations, such as under the ring road, to separate bicycles from motorized vehicles traveling at higher speeds, improving the safety of bicyclists.

> **BOX 8.3 VINEX LOCATIONS**
> Vinex locations are areas in the Netherlands, generally in the outskirts of cities, designated for housing development. The program was created by the Dutch Ministry of Housing in 1993 as an answer to the anticipated housing shortage, mainly due to the high growth rate of the population. More than just an urban-extension program, the Vinex project was intended to metamorphose the shape of the Netherlands. Over a million houses were to be built by 2015, in new neighborhoods fulfilling special conditions. "To fit the requirements of the consumer in the 21st century," special attention was given to quality, sustainability and social equity.
>
> The principles of Vinex housing are:
>
> - Build cohesive neighborhoods in place of existing urban gaps to reduce the fragmentation of Dutch cities and to protect green areas.
> - Make easily accessible all urban facilities and, in particular, shopping centers in order to increase the potential customer base.
> - Reduce car dependency by providing easy access to urban facilities by public transportation or non-motorized transportation.
> - Build a viable and social structure that will correspond to all layers of society.
>
> Vinex locations are required to create growth plans following certain standards. To avoid segregation, 30 percent of housing is required to be social housing, which is subsidized by the government and meant for low-income households. Additionally, housing must be high-density, with at least 12 houses per acre, must conform to market conditions, must maintain the relation between existing and new urban areas, and must use sustainable design (http://vinex-locaties.nl/).

In 1994, Houten was again designated as a new growth area under the government's new urban expansion program called Vinex (see Box 8.3). Plans were made to replicate the Houten model directly to the south, forming the city of South Houten. A second train station was constructed, also surrounded by a ring road, linked to the ring road of Houten, forming the southern part of the figure eight. The link between the ring roads is slightly elevated and has three bicycle and pedestrian underpasses so that the original Houten and South Houten are well connected by bike.

To this day, city policies in Houten have a strong focus on bicycle safety and bicycle rights. The local bicyclist union is also very active in advocating for bicycle infrastructure and bicycle rights.

KEY POLICY AND DESIGN STRATEGIES

Sustainable transportation is one of the main priorities of the City of Houten. Beyond its emphasis on urban design focused on bicyclists and pedestrians, the city has also applied several other policy and design measures, the combination of which has had a great impact on travel behavior of its citizens. These are described below.

Bicycle and pedestrian infrastructure

The city of Houten has over eight miles of bicycle paths, which are colored brick-red. In the city center, these paths are completely separated from car traffic, although motorized scooters are allowed to use them. This is due to a Dutch ruling that places low-speed scooters in the same category as bicycles. Therefore, these motorized scooters can legally not be excluded from using the paths. In order to improve safety, speed bumps are located on bicycle paths throughout the city designed specifically to slow motorized scooters while providing minimal disturbance to bicyclists. The entrance to many of the bicycle paths is blocked by bollards, so cars are physically unable to enter these pathways, although many are being removed to prevent bicyclists from getting injured by riding into them.

Photo 8.1

Bicyclist in Houten

Photo 8.2

Bicycle path in Houten

Photo 8.3

Speed bumps designed to slow motorized scooters but not bikes in Houten

The majority of roadways within the city are shared between bikes and cars. Traffic speeds are very low due to design features built into the roadway design, including narrow streets and turns every 250 feet, forcing drivers to slow to maneuver the curves. Furthermore, signs are located on select streets, particularly those near schools, stating that cars are "guests" on the road and must give priority to bicyclists. Bicycle tunnels and bridges have been built under or over the ring roads so that neither bicycle nor car traffic are interrupted, and to make it easier for bicyclists to get out to the country. In addition, bicycle paths connect Houten to the City of Utrecht, and other neighboring communities, where many residents commute for work.

This extensive focus on bicycle priority above the car and slow traffic speeds on all city streets is unique to the City of Houten. Furthermore, infrastructure costs for Houten are no higher than for any other Vinex location in the Netherlands (Beaujon 2002; Tiemens 2010). This focus makes bicycling in Houten easier, safer and more convenient than in other cities. Surveys have shown that even those not predisposed to bicycling bike more as a result of living in Houten (Hilbers 2008). This demonstrates the strong impact infrastructure and roadway design can have on travel choices.

One issue encountered is that since so many residents bike, it can often be difficult to find a bicycle parking spot, especially in high-trafficked areas such as the city center. To resolve this issue, the city recently constructed a staffed bicycle parking facility and bicycle shop under the tracks of the central train station. This helped to relieve bike parking capacity issues in the city and also greatly reduced bike thefts in the city center.

8: THE RANDSTAD: HOUTEN CASE STUDY

Photo 8.4 *(top left)*

Sign stating that bikes have priority and cars are "guests" in Houten

Photo 8.5 *(top right)*

Bicycle tunnel under ring road in Houten

Photo 8.6 *(right)*

Bicycle paths and crowded bike parking in Houten

Photo 8.7

Bicycle paths around residential neighborhood in Houten

Urban design

Houten's early focus on urban design is a key to the city's current level of transportation sustainability. When designing the city, Houten's planning advisors considered how the location of housing and layout of roads and bicycle paths would affect resident travel behavior. They did not neglect the car in their designs, but created a layout that would give priority to bicyclists.

Street layout and design

The street network in Houten consists of north and south ring roads joining to form a figure eight, each with a radius of about one half-mile. From the ring road, there are roads leading to every residence; however, generally there are no direct links between neighborhoods by car. In order to access another neighborhood or the city center, drivers must first enter the ring road and then exit again at their destination. However, due to applications of filtered permeability, bikes have direct access points between neighborhoods. This layout provides easy access to the freeway for cars, but encourages biking and walking within the city. For example, from the ring road, there are only two access points for cars to the city center, where the majority of supermarkets, cafes and shops are, while there are direct access points by bike from every neighborhood. As a result, biking is often the fastest mode of travel for trips within the city.

Urban design features were used to mark the transitions from the ring road to the residential areas. By law, drivers are required to slow down when exiting the ring road, which has a speed limit of 56 mph, and entering the 20 mph residential areas, but these design features help to further ensure safety at ring road exits. First, tall buildings are located on either side of the access road at these transition points to act as a visual signal to drivers that they are entering the city. Additionally, there is a change in the road from asphalt pavement to bricks and a fork to slow down car speed. Furthermore, no residential street is straight for more than 250 feet, which helps to maintain safe vehicle speeds and heighten driver awareness of the surroundings.

Photo 8.8

Bicycle priority at intersection in Houten

PUBLIC SPACE DESIGN

The City of Houten has incorporated many open public spaces and green areas into its design. Next to the central train station is a plaza surrounded by a man-made canal and home to numerous shops and cafes. The plaza is often used for public markets, making it a bustling activity center. A similar plaza with shops and cafes, but incorporating a Romanesque theme, is planned for the Houten Castellum station in the south of the city. Many small play areas and parks are located throughout the city so that no one has to go far to find green space. In addition, a small forest, complete with bicycle paths and play areas for children, was created just outside the city. The objective was to create an area near the city, accessible by bicycle or walking, where residents could escape to enjoy nature without having to drive.

LAND USE PLANNING AND DESIGN

In the core of each of Houten's rings is a train station, so that no one lives more than a mile away from a station. Next to each station is a plaza with shops and other amenities. Housing is arranged "like petals of a flower" around these central areas (Beaujon 2002). This style follows the classic layout of a transit-oriented development (TOD), with housing and retail focused around a central transit station, maximizing access for all residents. Furthermore, the majority of schools and important buildings are located along a bicycle thoroughfare, which runs through the center of the city, providing easy access to important destinations by bike.

A business park is located in South Houten close to the border between the two rings, providing many job opportunities to residents. Total employment in Houten matches the number of workers almost exactly, providing job opportunities within Houten to residents. About one-third of Houten residents also work in the city, meaning that about two-thirds of employees in Houten come from elsewhere.

In addition, the historic village center of Houten is located in the southwestern part of the northern ring, which consists of a plaza surrounded by small shops and restaurants, as well as several historical buildings, including a Protestant church that dates back to the 1500s.

Photo 8.9

Bicyclists in central plaza in Houten

Public transportation

As mentioned, Houten has two railway stations, one located in the center of each ring: Houten Station and Houten Castellum Station. Every 15 minutes, a train takes travelers from both Houten stations to the City of Utrecht, with a journey time of 10 minutes. Utrecht is the hub of the Netherlands rail network, so there commuters can make easy connections to Amsterdam and other Dutch cities. There are also four trains per hour running in the opposite direction, towards the town of Geldermalsen. Houten also has bus connections to Utrecht and other regional centers. The trains and buses make it easy for residents to access Utrecht and other parts of the Netherlands without needing a car.

Train and bus riders in Houten may use the OV-chipkaart, a contactless smartcard that can be used on all public transport in the Netherlands. Introduction of this card simplifies the process of traveling to other parts of the country. The same card can also be used in the GWL Terrein development located in Amsterdam.

Public bikes

An OV-Fiets (translated as "public transport bicycle") rental station with 35 bikes is located at a staffed bicycle parking facility near Houten's central train station. OV-Fiets started as a pilot project in the Netherlands in 2002 with the aim to integrate bike rental as part of the services offered by the Dutch public transport system. There are now over 160 rental points, mainly located at train stations throughout the Netherlands. The scheme has been designed as a last-mile connection, to encourage bicycle use over motorized transportation for the last leg of a journey between the station and a destination not near transit. It is often used by business travelers who don't go to the same place daily, so they don't have a bike waiting for them. As of 2008, 50 percent of the nation's rail passengers had access to the scheme (OV-Fiets (NL) 2008).

OV-Fiets users must register with the system and a Dutch bank account is necessary for the subscription charges. Users can sign up using their existing annual rail card (much like the Oyster scheme in London). Each individual rental costs $3.50 per 24-hour period up to a maximum of 72 hours. The yearly subscription charge is $11. Members may use a bike at any location throughout the Netherlands, but must always return the bike to the station where it was obtained.

The OV-Fiets system differs from bike sharing systems being introduced in many cities, such as Velib in Paris, Stockholm City Bikes, and Bay Area Bike Share in the San Francisco area, in which short trips are encouraged and users can pick up and drop off bikes at numerous locations throughout the city. OV-Fiets, on the other hand, has one charge per 24-hour period, so users often keep the bikes for longer periods of time. Additionally, each bike comes equipped with a lock, making it possible for users to park the bike, for example, at their office during the day, and use the bike throughout the day for trips or errands. The bike must then be brought back to the same station where it was checked out. Therefore, it functions as a hybrid system between bike sharing and bicycle rental.

Photo 8.10

Carsharing vehicle in Houten

Carsharing
Two carsharing companies are located in Houten: Greenwheels (www.greenwheels.nl) and Wheels4All (www.wheels4all.nl). Greenwheels has two carsharing vehicles in Houten, one of which is located near the central station. Wheels4All has 14 cars located throughout the city. These vehicles provide residents of Houten with access to a car when needed without having to own one.

Employer contributions
In the Netherlands, many companies compensate employees for their transportation to work. This money is subsidized by the government through tax deductions. Typically, employers provide a variety of options that employees can choose between, such as reimbursement for fuel, free parking, transit passes and even providing money toward the purchase of a new bike. For example, one option for employees of the City of Houten is to purchase a tax-deductable bike every three years. Furthermore, the City of Houten varies from the national policy in that it does not allow companies to offer compensation options related to cars. Companies may only offer transportation subsidies related to bikes or public transit, in order to encourage employees to choose these options over commuting by car (Tiemens 2010).

Educational programs
Children are taught from an early age not only about the health benefits of bicycling, but also about bicycle safety. Since bicycling is a primary mode of transportation in Houten, it is essential that residents understand appropriate and safe bicycle use. Therefore, children are given a thorough education in bicycle riding and take a compulsory bicycle exam when they are 10 years old to test their knowledge of hand signals, road rules and riding ability. Furthermore, children continue to take this test until they pass (CylcePress 2003).

QUANTITATIVE ANALYSIS
In order to quantify the benefits of Houten's unique combination of urban design structure and policy measures, the city is compared to the City of Zeist, to provide a reference point within the Netherlands, and the city of Milton Keynes in England, to demonstrate the difference between bike-oriented and car-oriented urban design. Zeist has a similar population to Houten and, like Houten, is located on the outskirts of Utrecht (a regional center with a population of 310,000). Like many cities in the Netherlands, Zeist has good bicycle and pedestrian infrastructure; however, its street network is much more car-oriented than the Houten network. Milton Keynes, like Houten, was designed in the 1960s as a new city; it was

Table 8.1 Statistics for Houten, Zeist, Milton Keynes, South Houten and Veldhuizen

	Houten	Zeist	Milton Keynes	South Houten	Veldhuizen
Population	43,900	60,400	196,000	18,700	9,350
Urban area (acres)	2,030	6,200	22,000	860	470
Urban density (persons/acre)	22	10	9	22	20
Number of residential units	18,400	26,600	N/A	5,700	3,500
Cars per 1,000 residents	415	530	N/A	449	N/A
Mode share	*All trips*			*To work*	
Car	34%	46%	70%	58%	77%
Public transit	11%	11%	10%	16%	10%
Bicycle	28%	29%	3%	24%	13%
Walking	27%	14%	17%	2%	0%

Sources: ITDP (2010), City of Houten (www.houten.nl/), City of Zeist (www.zeist.nl/), Milton Keynes Council (2009), Hilbers (2008)

the last and largest of the British government's new towns, under the 1946 New Towns Act. The city is located about 50 miles northwest of London. Unlike Houten's bicycle- and pedestrian-focused, dense, urban design, Milton Keynes was designed with the car in mind, focusing on low densities and easy car access on high-speed grid roads. In a further attempt to accommodate the car, the parking supply is quite high, as much as two to three times higher than what would be expected for a city of its size (Whiteside 2007).

Additionally, the area of South Houten is compared to the neighborhood of Veldhuizen, located in the Leidsche Rijn district of the City of Utrecht. Like South Houten, Leidsche Rijn was identified as a high growth area, or Vinex location (see Box 8.3). Both locations were required to follow the same Vinex location guidelines, including reserving 30 percent of housing as social housing, providing a density of at least 12 houses per acre, maintaining the relation between existing and new urban areas and using sustainable design. The neighborhoods in the Leidsche Rijn district were designed individually, each with its own identity. However, the urban designers of Veldhuizen and other neighborhoods of Leidsche Rijn took a different approach to the planners of Houten, placing more focus on cars, and therefore providing more parking facilities and more main roads (Hilbers 2008). Veldhuizen is also less accessible to transit since the train station is located along the border of the neighborhood, rather than in the center, so some residents must travel up to two miles to reach the station while no one in South Houten lives more than a mile from the train station. Table 8.1 provides a summary of statistics for the entire City of Houten (within the two ring roads), the City of Zeist, the City of Milton Keynes, the area of South Houten (within the southern ring road) and the neighborhood of Veldhuizen.

Car and bicycle ownership rates

While the car ownership rate of Houten (415 cars per 1,000 residents) is not necessarily low compared to large cities such as Amsterdam, it is extremely low compared to other suburban cities, such as the nearby City of Zeist (530 cars per 1,000 residents). A survey of Milton Keynes residents found that 45 percent of households have two or more cars (Milton Keynes Council 2009). This is higher than for the City of Houten, where 36 percent of households have two or more cars (ITDP 2010). The Milton Keynes survey did not ask the exact number of cars owned by the household, so it is not possible to calculate the car ownership rate.

Surveys conducted in both Houten and Milton Keynes asked about the bicycle ownership rates for households. In Houten, only 2 percent of households are without a bicycle, while in Milton Keynes 35 percent of households do not own a bike. The bicycle ownership rate is quite high in Houten at 3.4 bikes per household. The rate is much lower in Milton Keynes at 1.1 bikes per household. This is

Figure 8.2

Activity level of residents of the Netherlands, South Houten and Veldhuizen

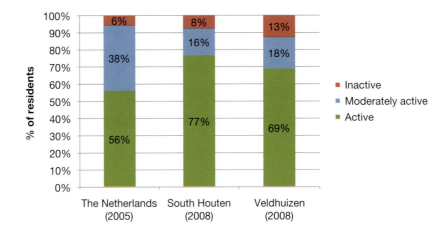

Figure 8.3

Perceptions of bicycle path quality and safety in South Houten and Veldhuizen

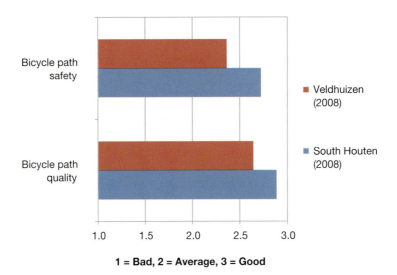

not surprising given that the Netherlands is known for having a much stronger bicycle culture than England. However, investments in bicycle infrastructure, such as grade-separated bike crossings, also likely contribute to this difference. Furthermore, the bicycle paths in Houten are direct and are perceived as safe by residents, while the bicycle lanes in Milton Keynes are not direct, can be difficult to follow and are perceived by some to be dangerous after dark (Whiteside 2007).

Bicycle use and perceptions

Results of a survey conducted by University of Utrecht students shows that people in South Houten are more active, on average, than people in both Veldhuizen and the Netherlands as a whole (Figure 8.2). Factors contributing to this increased activity are that residents of South Houten more often bicycle for daily and weekly errands and also spend more hours per week on recreational cycling (2.3 hours per week for South Houten residents versus 1.4 hours per week for Veldhuizen residents). It would appear that the spatial design structure and extensive bicycle network seem to encourage bicycling in Houten. This is further supported by survey findings that residents of South Houten are more satisfied with the number of unhindered bike paths and give higher ratings for quality and safety of bike paths (Figure 8.3). In addition, more than half of the survey respondents stated that their bicycle use increased after moving to South Houten (Hilbers 2008).

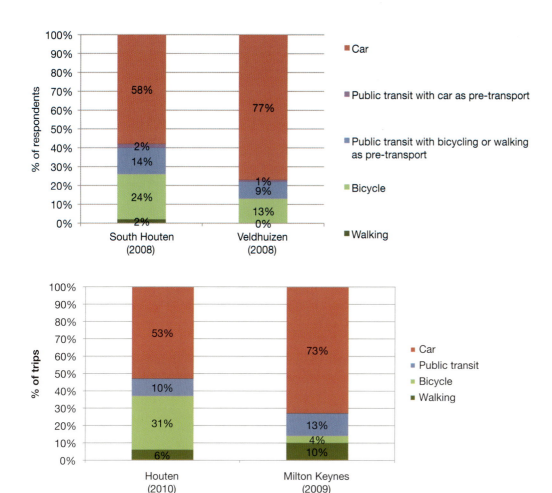

Figure 8.4

Mode of travel to work for South Houten and Veldhuizen residents

Figure 8.5

Mode of travel to work for Houten and Milton Keynes residents

Mode split

While it is apparent that residents of Houten do more recreational bicycling than residents in surrounding areas, a key to reducing the carbon footprint of residents is to shift necessary trips (such as work and shopping trips) from motorized modes to non-motorized modes. A survey of South Houten and Veldhuizen residents in 2008 found that more respondents from South Houten (24 percent) bike to work than respondents from Veldhuizen (13 percent), as seen in Figure 8.4. Furthermore, 14 percent of respondents from South Houten bike or walk to a public transportation stop or station and then take public transportation to work versus 9 percent in Veldhuizen. A far smaller proportion of South Houten residents (58 percent) travel to work by car than Veldhuizen residents (77 percent).

Surveys of residents of Houten and Milton Keynes found that far more work trips made by Houten residents (31 percent) are by bike than work trips made by Milton Keynes residents (4 percent), as seen in Figure 8.5. In addition, far more commute trips by Milton Keynes residents (73 percent) are by car than in Houten (53 percent). This demonstrates that Milton Keynes residents are much more dependent on their cars for work trips than Houten residents.

Still, many work trips made by Houten residents are by car, particularly for trips out of the city. However, by far, the most popular mode of travel for trips made within the city is bicycling. The majority of Houten residents travel to the grocery store (53 percent), conduct other shopping (70 percent), run service-related errands such as visiting the bank or barber (79 percent) and visit friends and family in Houten (79 percent) by bike or on foot, as seen in Figure 8.6.

8: THE RANDSTAD: HOUTEN CASE STUDY

Figure 8.6

Mode of travel for various trip types for Houten residents (2010)

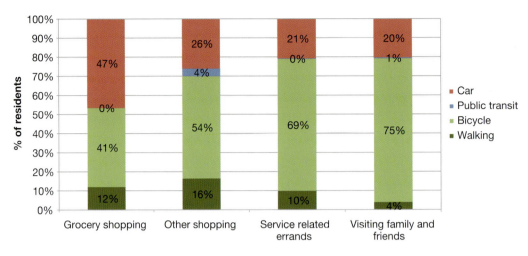

Figure 8.7

Mode of travel for all trips made by Houten, Zeist and Milton Keynes residents

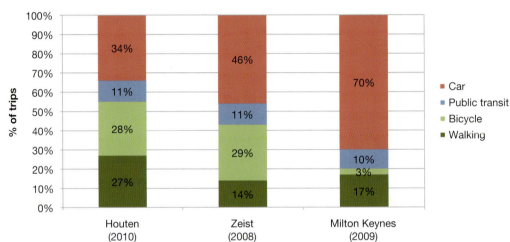

Overall, more than half of all trips made by Houten residents (55 percent) are made by non-motorized modes of travel, which is higher than for the City of Zeist (43 percent) and Milton Keynes (20 percent). Further, higher proportions of trips made by Milton Keynes (70 percent) and Zeist residents (46 percent) are by car than for the City of Houten (34 percent), as seen in Figure 8.7. A further study found that 42 percent of trips shorter than five miles in Houten are made by bike, and around 21 percent by foot (www.houten.nl/). Another study states that car use in Houten is 25 percent lower than in similar cities (Beaujon 2002). All of these studies support the finding that the combination of measures present in Houten have contributed to improved sustainability of travel choices of residents, particularly for trips within the city.

Distance traveled

Distance traveled is a key measure for evaluating transport-related emissions. Resident surveys found that residents of South Houten have shorter commute times than residents of Veldhuizen, even while more people commute to work by bike and fewer by car. This suggests that residents of South Houten live closer to work, thus requiring less daily travel, and reducing the carbon footprint of residents (Hilbers 2008).

Indeed, surveys of residents throughout the City of Houten found that 21 percent of residents live within three miles of their place of work or education, and more than half live within 10 miles. However, the finding that almost half of residents live 10 miles or more from their place or work corresponds with

8: THE RANDSTAD: HOUTEN CASE STUDY

Photo 8.11

Bicycle trailer in Houten

the finding that 53 percent of resident commute trips are by car (Figure 8.5). For longer travel distances, residents are forced to travel by motorized modes since most are not able to bike or walk such long distances. While the train is competitive for longer trips to certain destinations such as the center of Utrecht or Amsterdam, the car is much more convenient for others such as the University of Utrecht or nearby cities such as Nijmegen. As a result, many residents still choose to travel by car to work, particularly for destinations more than 15 miles from home. Increased car travel increases the carbon footprint of residents.

Half of Houten residents travel less than a half-mile to their grocery store, and 18 percent travel one-third mile or less. The average distance residents travel to a grocery store is three-fourths of a mile (ITDP 2010). However, 47 percent of residents stated that they typically travel to the grocery store by car (Figure 8.6). Residents might be incentivized to drive to the store based on the low parking rates in parking garages in Houten and the high availability of parking spaces. If parking prices were increased, more residents would likely shift to biking to the grocery store, since the majority of residents already bike for most other trip purposes within the city (Figure 8.6). Indeed, many residents own bike trailers that can be used to carry goods. These trailers, combined with the short distance to a grocery store, make shopping trips by bicycle feasible.

LESSONS LEARNED

When taking measures to encourage sustainable transportation use, it is crucial to plan appropriately for their capacity. One issue encountered in the City of Houten is that since so many people bike, bicycle parking facilities quickly fill to capacity and residents complain about lack of bicycle parking. The City of Houten is aware of this issue and has recently constructed a staffed bicycle parking facility combined with a bicycle shop and bicycle repair services under the tracks of the central train station.

The demand for trains leaving from Houten's central station was also underestimated. As a result, frequency of train service to Houten was increased and the number of tracks on the line from Utrecht to the south via Houten was doubled to four tracks.

An important policy strategy not applied in Houten is to restrict parking by limiting and pricing parking. There is more than one parking space per residential unit in Houten. As a result, the majority of households own cars and the car ownership rate in the city is high compared to our other case study sites. In addition, two parking garages are located near the central station. The first two hours are free within these garages, then $2 per hour is charged up to a maximum of $10 per day. The shop owners in central Houten subsidize the free hours through their rent. They were worried they would lose business if people had to pay too much for parking (Tiemens 2010). However, as shown in Figure 8.6, most residents of Houten already walk or ride a bike for shopping trips, so parking prices could easily be raised without hurting business. Though most do bike, the low prices for parking might encourage some residents to drive to the grocery store rather than bike, even though they live within biking distance of the store.

Other cities that choose to replicate Houten's model should limit or economically decouple residential parking in order to encourage reduced car ownership. In addition, nonresidential parking should be priced in order to encourage residents to use other forms of transportation besides driving to do their shopping.

The higher car ownership rates of Houten remind us of the need to think about connectivity. Good intention for the internal design of a car-free or car-lite, low carbon community can only go so far. The regional connectivity to jobs and activity centers must also be taken into account. In the case of Houten, its position in the Randstadt affords great rail transit access to some of the urban centers such as Utrecht and Amsterdam, but jobs are scattered throughout the vast metropolitan region. In a sense, this is a variation on the problems we see in Los Angeles, stemming from a polynucleated city.

These seven case studies have provided a variety of examples of car-free and car-lite low carbon communities. From the car-free brownfield developments of GWL Terrein and Vauban, to the car-lite freeway redevelopment of Market and Octavia, to the showcase, former industrial port redevelopments of Hammarby Sjöstad, Västra Hamnen and Greenwich Millennium Village, to the suburban, masterplanned, greenfield development of Houten. The next section will compare and contrast the case studies and provide lessons learned for creating successful low carbon communities.

NOTE
1 See: www.youtube.com/watch?v=p4QT5rvnfS0.

REFERENCES

Beaujon, O. (2002) *Biker's Paradise: Houten*, Bike Europe.
CylcePress (2003) "Taking a look at Houten City," *CylcePress*, 189, May 2003.
Hilbers, B. (2008) *The Influence of the Spatial Planning on Bicycle Use and Health: Comparisons between Houten and Leidsche Rijn*, Amsterdam: University of Amsterdam.
ITDP (2010) Internet-based survey of Houten residents, conducted in cooperation with the City of Houten.
Milton Keynes Council (2009) *Milton Keynes Multi-Modal Transport Model: Report of Survey*, London: Halcrow Group.
OV-Fiets (NL (2008) *Bikeoff Project: Design Against Crime*, available at: www.bikeoff.org/design_resource/dr_PDF/schemes_public_Ov_fiets.pdf (accessed July 2015).
Rijkswaterstaat Centre for Transport and Navigation (2008).
Tiemens, H. (2010) Interview with Herbert Tiemens, Traffic Planner, City of Houten, May 27, 2010.
Whiteside, K. (2007) "MK transport: moving with the times," *Urban Design*, 104: 27–33.

9
Conclusions and lessons learned

INTRODUCTION

The seven case studies presented here have demonstrated that new developments can be built to facilitate the use of sustainable transportation, reducing the impacts of traffic congestion, greenhouse gases and other pollution, and creating opportunities for healthier modes of travel. This chapter provides a comparative analysis of the case study sites and recaps the lessons learned, looking at the larger context for the success of these projects, the potential for transferability to other North American and global cities, and makes policy recommendations for the future.

COMPARATIVE ANALYSIS

In order to better understand the potential transferability of the strategies presented in these case studies, it is worth revisiting some of the basic characteristics of each of the sites, including size, density and distance from the city center. These are shown in Table 9.1.

Comparison of site characteristics

Some key characteristics to highlight include the following. First, the sizes and locations of these developments do vary. GWL Terrein is relatively small compared to Hammarby Sjöstad and Market and Octavia, while Houten is an entire city of almost 50,000 inhabitants. Also, some sites (such as Västra Hamnen) are located much closer to the city center than other sites (such as Greenwich Millennium Village). It is important to keep these differences in mind as they can affect the results of the measures applied, as well as highlighting the importance of location and city size in increasing the propensity to use non-motorized modes. Moreover, all the sites have unique characteristics, meaning that care should be taken to ensure comparisons of basic descriptive statistics are meaningful.

Table 9.1 Summary of site characteristics

City	Development	Current population	Developed area (acres)	Residential units	Population density (persons/acre)	Parking spaces per residential unit	Distance from city center (miles)
Amsterdam	GWL Terrein	1,400	15	600	95	0.22	1.8
Freiburg	Vauban	5,500	100	2,470	55	< 0.5	2
San Francisco	Market and Octavia	30,800	740	19,100	42	< 0.6	1.5
Stockholm	Hammarby Sjöstad	20,000	400	10,000	50	0.65	2
Malmö	Västra Hamnen	7,000	215+	4,000	33	0.8	1.2
London	Greenwich Millennium Village	2,300	50+	1,095	46	0.7	5
Houten	Houten	48,000	2,030	18,400	24	1.1	5*

* Distance from Utrecht city center + Plus current developed area

Table 9.2 Overview of urban design and policy features

Development	Lesson 1 Parking reform	Lesson 2 Automobile restraint	Lesson 2 Pedestrian/bicycle infrastructure	Lesson 3 Public transit provision	Lesson 4 Distance from city center (miles)	Lesson 5 Residential density (persons/acre)	Mix of land uses	Lesson 6 Process	Lesson 7 Policy
GWL Terrein	Limited, spatially separated, rationed	Entire site is car-free	High quality	High provision	1.8	95	High diversity	Car-free declaration, residents association	Environmental requirements
Vauban	Limited, priced, spatially separated	Mostly car-free	High quality	High provision	2	55	High diversity	Car-free declaration, residents association	Minimum parking standards
Market and Octavia	Limited, priced	No car restrictions, major through traffic	Limited connectivity	High provision	1.5	42	High diversity	Citizen advisory committee	Environmental requirements, developer contributions
Hammarby Sjöstad	Limited, priced	No car restrictions	High quality	High provision	2	50	High diversity	None	Environmental requirements
Västra Hamnen	Limited, priced	Bo01 is car-free, others areas are not	High quality	High provision	1.2	33	High diversity	Mobility management	Environmental requirements, mobility goals
Greenwich Millennium Village	Limited, priced, spatially separated	Mostly car-free	Limited connectivity	High provision	5	46	Medium diversity	None	Developer contributions, sustainability goals
Houten	Not limited	Limited vehicle access between neighborhoods	High quality	High provision	5*	24	Some segregation of uses	Educational programs	Environmental requirements, employer contributions

* Distance from Utrecht city center

9: CONCLUSIONS AND LESSONS LEARNED

Table 9.3 Mode share and car ownership rates for study sites and reference areas

Location	Cars per 1,000 residents	Mode share (proportion of all trips) (%)			
		By car	By transit	By bicycle	On foot
GWL Terrein	190	6%	14%	50%	30%
Amsterdam West	310	20%	18%	32%	30%
Vauban^	172	16%	19%	64%+	
Rieselfeld^	320	30%	25%	52%+	
Market and Octavia*	400	35%	40%	7%	17%
The Marina*	650	50%	31%	2%	15%
Hammarby Sjöstad	210	21%	52%	9%	18%
Stockholm reference district	N/A	35%	50%	7%	8%
Västra Hamnen	440	23%	17%	31%	29%
City of Malmö	480	41%	16%	23%	20%
Greenwich Millennium Village	350	18%	49%	4%	29%
Greenwich District	350	44%	29%	1%	26%
City of Houten	415	34%	11%	28%	27%
City of Zeist (the Netherlands)	530	46%	11%	29%	14%

^ Mode share data from 1999/2000 (prior to extension of the tram system to Vauban)

+ Combined bicycle and walk mode share (data for bicycle and walk mode shares separated were not available)

* Commute mode share, on foot includes walking and telecommuting (since data on mode share for all trips were not available for San Francisco, commute mode share is used as a proxy)

Comparison of design and policy measures

A variety of policy and design measures were implemented in each of the case study sites. Table 9.2 summarizes the key measures and compares them on a high-level scale: green being a best practice application of the measure, yellow being a good application and orange representing a lack of application or room for improvement. For continuity and convenience, we have organized the table to correspond with the lessons learned described in the following section.

As shown, GWL Terrein is green in every category and is the case study we would recommend others strive toward. However, the smaller scale of the project, coupled with its excellent site and situation in one of the world's most bicycle-friendly cities, is something other cities do not have. Thus, our emphasis is on "strive."

Quantifying success

As we have shown in each of the case studies, the policy and design measures to reduce automobile dependency are generally working. Car ownership rates, mode share, car usage and transport-related emissions are lower in the case study developments than in comparable reference sites. Table 9.3 compares mode share and car ownership rates between each case study site and a reference site, while Figure 9.1 shows a comparison of transport-related emissions of four of the case study sites.

CAR OWNERSHIP RATES

First and foremost, per capita car ownership is an important indicator because if a resident does not have a car or have access to a car, he or she simply must use other forms of transportation. The car ownership rate per 1,000 residents varies greatly between the various sites. Vauban has the lowest car ownership rate with 172 cars per 1,000 residents, followed closely by GWL Terrein with 190 cars per

9: CONCLUSIONS AND LESSONS LEARNED

Figure 9.1

Land transport-related emissions comparisons

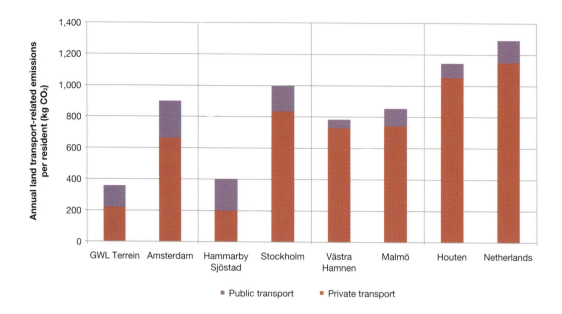

1,000 residents. These results show that car-free developments, where parking spaces are extremely limited and separated from residential units, have very low car ownership rates. This may be due in part to the self-selecting nature of residents who choose to live in a car-free environment. However, while it is unclear the degree to which such sites influence the behavior of residents, simply providing the opportunity for residents to live car-free has the potential to create neighborhoods with low car ownership rates, catalyzing car-free or car-lite lifestyles. In contrast, areas that do not restrict parking have a smaller impact on encouraging reduced car ownership; for example, Houten has 415 cars per 1,000 residents. This is relatively higher than most of our case studies, but still, this value is lower than in many other areas where few or no policy and design measures have been implemented.

Mode share

Although car ownership rate is an important indicator, it does not paint the full picture. For example, in Houten, the car is not used for all trips, nor necessarily the majority of trips. Many of the parking and traffic-calming strategies applied attempt to encourage residents to use sustainable forms of transportation, particularly for short trips. For all of the sites, the private motorized vehicle mode share is less than 35 percent, meaning the majority of trips are made by other modes. Furthermore, all of the sites have a lower private motorized vehicle mode share than reference sites, which do not have the policy and design measures found in the case studies.

GWL Terrein has an especially notable mode share: 30 percent of all trips taken by residents are on foot, 50 percent by bike, 14 percent by public transit and only 6 percent by car. Houten and Västra Hamnen also have high non-motorized mode shares. In Houten, 27 percent of trips are made on foot and 28 percent by bike. In Västra Hamnen, 29 percent of trips are made on foot and 31 percent by bike. These results demonstrate that even in areas where car ownership is relatively high, residents may choose to make a majority of trips by non-motorized modes. Likewise, among Vauban's car-owning population, 61 percent of commuting and daily shopping trips are made by bicycle. These choices are likely influenced by the comprehensive application of policy and design measures in these locations. As the analysis of Houten shows, most trips made within the city appear to be made by bike or walking. However, the higher car ownership rate leads to longer trips being made by car.

In San Francisco and London, comparatively low rates of bicycling reflect each case study's lack of a comprehensively connected bicycle system, compounded in the case of Market and Octavia, by the high traffic density. Contrasting that, the transit and walking shares are relatively high in these two developments, in part because infrastructure is in place.

9: CONCLUSIONS AND LESSONS LEARNED

CARBON EMISSIONS

While mode share gives a general idea of resident travel behavior, it cannot be used to accurately calculate CO_2 emissions. For four of the sites studied, data on average distance traveled per mode per resident were collected by travel surveys conducted by ITDP in 2010. (San Francisco emissions data were not available at the scale of the Market and Octavia neighborhood, so we were unable to evaluate the emissions, but lower VMT rates suggest lower emissions.)

A simple estimate was made of transport-related emissions per resident per year by multiplying average distance traveled per motorized mode (including both private and public transport) by emissions estimates per passenger-mile traveled for each mode. A more rigorous CO_2 evaluation would consider the effect of vehicle speed and trip length on CO_2 emission rate per passenger-mile traveled, which would reflect the higher CO_2 intensity per passenger-mile traveled for short motor vehicle trips. Figure 9.1 shows a breakdown of emissions from private transport (for example, cars) and public transport (for example, bus, train, tram, metro), and compares emissions between the four case study sites and the city or country in which they are located. From this figure, we can see that there is a relationship between car ownership rate and emissions from private transport. Private transport emissions are much lower in GWL Terrein and Hammarby Sjöstad, where car ownership rates are low, than in Västra Hamnen and Houten, where car ownership rates are higher. Even though non-motorized mode share in Västra Hamnen and Houten are high, it appears that residents drive for many long trips and these passenger-miles traveled increase the carbon footprint of residents. Furthermore, transport-related emissions per resident are much lower for GWL Terrein and Hammarby Sjöstad than for the cities in which they are located (Amsterdam and Stockholm). However, transport-related emissions per resident for Västra Hamnen are similar to those for Malmö, and emissions for Houten residents are similar to those for the Netherlands.

In the case of San Francisco, we can consider lower household VMT as a proxy for lower emissions, and infer that because Market and Octavia has a household VMT ranging between 1 and 10 vehicle miles per day per household, the plan is successful when compared to the regional planning goal of achieving between 30 and 40 VMT per day in 2035 (which is considered adequate for reaching regional transportation emissions targets, although this is debatable and was challenged by environmental organizations when the regional plan was adapted in 2013).

LESSONS FOR SMART URBAN GROWTH: POLICY AND DESIGN STRATEGIES

Each of the lessons described here refers to a corresponding column or pair of columns in Table 9.2.

Lesson 1: reforming parking and implementing auto restraint

Car ownership and use can be reduced significantly through a reduction in parking supply, combined with the spatial and fiscal separation of the parking that is provided. Low speed limits, traffic calming and filtered permeability further decrease the speed and convenience of car travel. These factors encourage residents to consider whether car ownership is necessary to meet everyday mobility needs, and if so whether it is the most convenient mode for local trips. The provision of carsharing is helpful for any strategy designed to reduce car ownership. However, the most critical policy for U.S. cities is to eliminate parking minimums and replace them with parking maximums that are organized to discourage excessive car ownership and use.

Parking

All but one of the sites have limited parking, some to less than 0.5 spaces per residential unit. Houten is the exception, and consequently has one of the highest car ownership rates. In Market and Octavia, the cumulative parking ratio for newly constructed and pipeline projects is between 0.5 and 0.6 parking spaces per residential unit, and several new developments are 100 percent car-free, with more in the pipeline. Household car ownership rates have remained stable or declined, and are lower than in other neighborhoods, reflecting success compared to other parts of San Francisco.

On-site parking is managed in the case study sites via techniques including limiting parking, pricing parking and separating residential units from car parking through spatial and/or economic decoupling.

Spatially separating parking spaces from residential units makes car use less convenient in general, and particularly so for short trips that can easily be made by walking or bicycling. This is a key strategy for the car-free developments of GWL Terrein and Vauban, in which all or most parking is located on the side of the development, away from residences. As a result, most residents actually live closer to a public transit stop than to peripheral parking.

Economically decoupling (unbundling) parking spaces from residential units by requiring residents to purchase parking spaces separately from housing units makes residents aware of the actual land value of parking spaces, and may discourage them from owning a car. Parking spaces must be purchased or rented in Greenwich Millennium Village, in new developments in Market and Octavia, and in Vauban. These fees are unbundled from property/apartment rental prices, with upfront costs of up to $30,000 per car. Legal frameworks for the effective enforcement of parking restrictions are likely to be required if the German "car-free declaration" model, in which an exemption from having to pay for parking is granted only for those without a car, is to be adopted elsewhere.

In most of the other sites studied, residents may park in the surrounding area by purchasing a residential parking permit. The price and number of residential parking permits can be set to discourage vehicle ownership, and controlled parking zones or other measures are required to prevent car owners from parking in adjacent areas.

Appropriate pricing for public on-street and off-street (garage) parking can also encourage visitors to come via sustainable modes of travel. Generally, it is recommended to charge more for on-street parking than for off-street parking to encourage long-term parkers to park in garages, providing faster turnover of on-street spaces.

Automobile restraint

Restricting car access is another strategy to deter car use. Most of the sites studied have at least partially car-free zones. GWL Terrein is entirely car-free: no cars are permitted on-site. GWL Terrein has avoided Vauban's problem of illegal parking in "parking-free" streets by making internal paths narrower and physically barring access to almost all motor vehicles. Through traffic is prevented in Vauban by providing access to motor vehicles at only one location, whereas pedestrians and bicyclists may reach neighboring districts and the city center directly via several access points. An exception to this is Market and Octavia, which is situated at the crossroads of major arterials and faces ongoing traffic challenges. Traffic calming is a front-burning issue and the citizen advisory commission has prioritized a set of traffic calming measures such as pedestrian bulb-outs and "day lighting" of intersections by removing parked cars—a tactic to increase pedestrian visibility and safety.

COMPLEMENTARY MEASURES IN THE WIDER AREA

Car use can also be discouraged through pricing and access restrictions in the wider area. Examples covered in the case studies include indirect driving routes in Houten, the exclusion of cars in Freiburg's historic city center, the central London and Stockholm congestion charges and expensive, limited parking in London and Amsterdam ($6 per hour in central Amsterdam). In San Francisco, new policies limiting right turns or forcing right turns keeps private cars from overwhelming Market Street and make it less attractive for commuting, and parking limits in commercial buildings downtown discourage driving to office buildings. Common to all of these policies is a reduction in the convenience of the automobile, whether this is in terms of time, trip costs or the availability of parking.

Lesson 2: making it easy for walking and bicycling

The flip side of automobile restraint is the ease of walking and bicycling. This includes creating high-quality infrastructure for bicyclists and pedestrians, and also designing a dense network of streets and paths that make walking and bicycling safer, easier and more comfortable. However, in order to facilitate a significant shift in trips to walking and bicycling, this network must be part of a comprehensive network of bicycle and pedestrian paths throughout the city, connecting people to the places they want to go. The GMV case study shows us that although internally the site has good bicycle and pedestrian infrastructure, the connectivity of the pedestrian and bicycle network outside of the development is more limited, reducing the number of walk and bike trips made from the development to shopping and job opportunities outside the development.

WALKING

Location and density both affect the convenience of walking. But high-quality design, including provision of safe and attractive walking routes as well as public spaces in which people want to spend time, is also essential. Vauban features covered arcades for pedestrians along the central avenue, while the Swedish sites studied offer waterfront promenades. The Market and Octavia Plan included reintroducing key crosswalks that had been removed half a century earlier in order to make it easier to drive.

All internal pathways are for the exclusive use of pedestrians and bicyclists in GWL Terrein, while Greenwich Millenium Village, Västra Hamnen and Vauban exclude cars from parts of the site, offering safe, quiet walking routes. Although slow to be deployed, the Market and Octavia Plan calls for a system of shared "living alleys" (often referred to as the woonerf concept, particularly in Europe), where cars are slowed to the speed of pedestrians and space is converted from parking to social gathering spaces.

9: CONCLUSIONS AND LESSONS LEARNED

Bicycling

Bicycling similarly requires good infrastructure on-site and in the wider area: on- and off-road bicycle lanes, plentiful, secure and covered bicycle parking (including at transit stops, workplaces and shops). Low speed limits are essential to encourage on-road bicycle use: a maximum of 30 km/hour (approximately 20 mph) is common to many of the case studies permitting car access, reduced further to walking pace in Vauban's parking-free residential streets. Traffic calming through street furniture, speed humps, frequent crosswalks, traffic diverters, narrow streets, partial closures and differently colored surfaces reinforces the message that priority should be given to pedestrians and bicyclists. All things considered, Houten is the standard for a bicycle-oriented development, while Market and Octavia reflects a site with a considerable way to go. If traffic calming is successfully implemented in Market and Octavia in a way that substantially reduces traffic density, it is expected that bicycling will increase.

Filtered permeability is employed in Vauban and Houten, with the latter taking the concept to its logical conclusion by providing a fine-grained network of direct, high-quality bicycle routes (including dedicated tunnels and bridges) that make bicycling quicker than the car for many journeys within the city. Bicyclists have priority on all streets shared with cars and at junctions where bicycle-only streets cross them. Streets are designed for slow speeds and intermittent signs remind users that cars are permitted "as guests."

Further measures to promote bicycling include an on-site bicycle workshop with free servicing in Vauban. Bike sharing systems have been implemented in several of the case study cities. Additionally, bicycles can be taken on board transit services in many of the cities studied, helping to extend the range of bicycle-transit trips and encouraging bike use in bad weather.

Lesson 3: prioritize transit

High-quality, accessible public transportation is key to encouraging use of this mode over the car. Ideally, these facilities are established in advance of construction of new developments, and, in some cases, such as in Greenwich Millennium Village, developers may be asked to provide funding for or construct new stops as part of the overall development. In Market and Octavia, development impact fees can be directed at Muni bus stops and also vehicle procurement.

All the case study sites benefit from a maximum distance of 1,500 feet from residential units to transit stops and daytime frequencies of at least 15 minutes. Operating hours are long and comprehensive, and information is provided at stops. Integrated transit agencies coordinate timetables and fares in all of the case study cities, ensuring connections are optimized and the "one trip, one ticket" principle applies. Orbital transit routes in the larger cities provide a realistic alternative to the car for complex trips other than to/from the city center. Transit priority measures in and around new developments maximize service reliability: trams in Freiburg, Stockholm and Vauban run largely on segregated rights of way. The Millennium Busway allows buses to avoid congestion as they pass through the GMV area. In San Francisco, new red carpet transit-only lanes speed bus service through the Market and Octavia area, and a new BRT line, currently under construction, will separate high-capacity bus service from car traffic.

And while it is unlikely that any one development can influence the ticking and payment systems for an entire transit system, the availability of smartcards and discount period passes in the areas studied do help make transit cheaper and more convenient.

Though these case studies have some of the best transit conditions, there is still room for improvement. In some areas, unstaffed stations with poorly lit approach routes and evidence of antisocial behavior such as graffiti make users feel unsafe. It is essential that transit feels safe, even at night, to reassure residents that they do not require their own car or taxis for these trips. Another issue in some of the sites is overcrowding on transit at peak times. In the Market and Octavia area, located between outer neighborhoods and downtown, transit is often already crowded as it moves through the neighborhood. There is large pent-up demand for transit, and studies show that improving transit reliability will draw even more ridership, resulting in more crowding. In that case, walking and bicycling options provide important relief to transit crowding. It is essential for planners to match transit demand and capacity or else other measures will be undermined.

CARSHARING

Carsharing is an intermediate public transit strategy. It is available in or around all of the sites studied: it should be considered a prerequisite for strategies to reduce private vehicle ownership, providing residents with a personal motorized transport option for occasional use. A variety of vehicle types is likely to boost the popularity of carsharing services. Bundling carsharing membership with transit passes (offered in Freiburg) offers a complete mobility package for residents without access to a household car. Discounted membership and/or rental rates can encourage take-up, as practiced in Västra Hamnen. New carsharing models are becoming more widely available including one-way carsharing models and peer-to-peer carsharing, increasing mobility options. In San Francisco, carsharing is also being located curbside, making it more visible and easier to access compared to car share pods hidden in the garages of new buildings.

Lesson 4: location

New developments should be planned as closely as possible to existing job centers and other destinations. Mixing land uses (housing, jobs, leisure facilities, shops, grocery stores, and so on) should be incorporated into new developments at the site selection and masterplanning stage to minimize travel distances, enabling residents to make routine trips on foot or by bicycle, with convenient public transportation offering a realistic alternative to the car. No amount of policy or design measures will work well if the new development is located far from jobs and services their residents need.

In many cities, this is difficult since urban areas are already built up, limiting potential for new development near city centers. Infill redevelopment provides opportunities for locating additional housing and services near existing job centers. The case studies demonstrate the potential for providing infill development on brownfield sites, particularly previously industrial waterfront ports, which are often near city centers, as was the case in Hammarby Sjöstad, Västra Hamnen and Greenwich Millennium Village. Urban freeway removal also opens opportunities for redevelopment near existing urban cores, as was demonstrated with Market and Octavia. Especially in U.S. suburbs, there is also tremendous opportunity to redevelop strip malls, shopping centers and other "greyfield" sites that could be stitched together into comprehensive infill corridors.

All of the sites studied are located close to a city center with a high concentration of job opportunities. GWL Terrein, Hammarby Sjöstad, Market and Octavia, Västra Hamnen and Vauban are located within two miles of city centers. Houten is five miles from the city center of Utrecht, its "parent city." Greenwich Millennium Village, the only case study located within a megacity, is three miles from the Canary Wharf financial district and around six miles from the City of London employment zone (the "Square Mile"). Market and Octavia is not only located adjacent to downtown San Francisco, but it is literally in the center of a diverse array of activity centers and destinations.

National and regional planning frameworks can be used to prioritize sustainable locations for development, as a prerequisite for reducing car use through policy and design measures, preferably on previously developed land within existing towns and cities. Peri-urban development at high densities in medium-size cities is the next best solution, provided that distances to centers of economic activity are small. It should be noted that the British "eco-towns" program (not studied in this report) received much criticism for failing to ensure the shortlisted sites were within easy reach of jobs, owing to their small size and the criterion that they should be physically separated from existing settlements. In the United States, removal of urban freeways provides opportunities for new urban development on valuable land, close to city centers. In Market and Octavia, seven acres of prime land opened up as a result of freeway removal, and additional potential exists as the city considers further freeway removal.

Lesson 5: compact, mixed use

Most of the sites studied are of sufficient size and density to sustain at least one supermarket, primary school and other vital services, all of which generate local employment, as well as frequent transit services. Notably, the heavily car-reduced development of GWL Terrein has a residential density of around 40 units per acre, this being made possible in part by building homes on land that would otherwise be used for parking.

Providing a mix of land uses reduces the need to travel by providing everyday goods and services within walking distance of residences. Planning regulations and guidance can promote or mandate mixed land use as part of the masterplanning process, as opposed to purely residential "commuter dormitories" that build in a need for daily travel by motorized modes. All of the sites studied either provide a mix of uses on-site or within easy walking distance of the development. Financial incentives can encourage businesses to locate in new developments, generating local job opportunities. For example, the City of Stockholm initially offered subsidies to encourage businesses to move into Hammarby Sjöstad. In Market and Octavia, zoning requires that all modest-sized new housing development also contain ground floor commercial space with the intention of activating the sidewalk and providing neighborhood services.

Although most of the case study sites fall short of theoretical self-sustainability in terms of jobs per resident, efforts have been made to provide additional on-site jobs in all of the sites. In addition, homeworking has been encouraged through the provision of "live/work" units and shared, serviced office space.

9: CONCLUSIONS AND LESSONS LEARNED

Lesson 6: process is important

PARTICIPATORY PLANNING
Residents and potential residents can also play a large part in shaping car-free or reduced car developments. GWL Terrein, Market and Octavia, and Vauban had citizen involvement from the initial masterplan consultation through to the creation of lobby groups to influence the masterplanning process, and even voluntary car-free declarations, as was the case in GWL Terrein. This grassroots pressure is important to supporting (or sometimes pushing) planning authorities to reduce and decouple parking. For example, the City of Freiburg does not officially support the principle of "parking-free" streets, preferring instead the Rieselfeld "carrots only" approach. However, experiences from GWL Terrein and Vauban demonstrate that sustained public support can influence the implementation of radical measures, such as car-free developments with reduced and decoupled parking. In Market and Octavia, continued citizen action has also successfully defended the reduced parking ratios in instances when developers sought excess parking. Further, a community advisory committee was established as stewards of the plan, with requirements that the committee include renters, low-income residents and merchants, along with homeowners.

EDUCATE AND INSPIRE
Ongoing marketing and travel awareness campaigns complement the provision of pedestrian, bicycle and transit infrastructure and services by promoting sustainable travel behavior in the long-term, especially where car ownership has not been reduced significantly.

Customized mobility advice is provided in Malmö, reinforced through incentives such as free bicycle use and discounted carshare membership. Residents of the first parking-free block to be built in Vauban were given free annual transit passes and rail discount cards upon moving in. Such transportation demand management measures are particularly effective if initiated when residents move into a new district. It is much harder to change travel behavior once residents have developed a routine of habitual car use.

Lesson 7: national (or state) policy context helps

Transportation policies at the city, regional and national levels play a key role in shaping daily travel behavior and residential location in the longer term. Congestion charges, priced and limited parking at destinations, high fuel prices, access restrictions, filtered permeability and high-quality transit all influence travel mode choice, reinforcing site-specific measures. All of the case study cities are served by national railroad systems, providing an alternative to the car for longer-distance journeys, thereby complementing measures to discourage car ownership and use in the local area. In Market and Octavia, rail service in the region (BART, Caltrain) and in Northern California (Amtrak California) are relatively good for the United States, but beyond the Northern California region, rail service is poor.

These developments were all created with a mandate to reduce or minimize driving. The reasons for the mandates may vary (to reduce CO_2 emissions, to limit the traffic impacts of these new developments, and so on), but the fact that they exist helps to provide political will for the urban planning and design decisions that follow. For example, in California, driving is connected to GHG reduction policies and regional planning. Growth is supposed to be steered toward compact, transit-oriented nodes, and the case study of Market and Octavia, although crafted in advance of the statewide legislation, has explicit language and policies encouraging living without a car. Such mandates can be codified, requiring caps on projected car trip generation and CO_2 emissions, or through conversion of parking minimums to parking maximums. Mandates can also be applied, requiring developers to fund or build transportation infrastructure and services (including transportation demand management services) as a condition of site approval, as was the case for Market and Octavia and Greenwich Millennium Village. Monitoring reports, such as the five-year benchmarking report for Market and Octavia, track the progress of plan implementation and provide empirical data to evaluate the efficacy of the mandates and codes.

Government policies

Two of the sites stand out for the use of formal mechanisms for the integration of more sustainable transportation policies into new developments: planning obligations (Section 106 agreements) in England and the California Environmental Quality Act (CEQA) in California. The former were introduced in the Town and Country Planning Act of 1990, facilitating negotiations between local planning authorities and developers to offset the negative impacts of new development, such as the loss of green space and traffic generation. This system is used to obtain financial or in-kind contributions "directly related to the scale and nature of development" from developers. It is typically used to deliver access roads and other infrastructure such as parks, bicycle parking, community centers and even schools, as well as revenue support for new transit services and funding for smart measures such as personalized travel planning. Full planning permission is granted only upon the completion of these Section 106 negotiations.

CEQA, passed in the state of California in 1970, similar to Section 106 agreements, requires state and local agencies within California to follow a protocol of analysis and public disclosure of environmental impacts of proposed projects and adopt all feasible measures to mitigate those impacts. The state of California has the strictest environmental policies in this regard, stricter than the National Environmental Policy Act (NEPA), also enacted in 1970.

Furthermore, in California, restrictions and caps on local government property taxes have led to greater reliance on development impact fees to finance infrastructure that aligns with new growth. Based on a nexus study, the Market and Octavia Plan area has a schedule of impact fees on all new residential and commercial projects, and these revenues are directed toward transit, pedestrian improvements, green spaces and other purposes.

In contrast, in Germany government policies have made integration of sustainable transportation policies more difficult. Minimum parking standards at the federal and regional levels thwarted attempts to eliminate parking from Vauban, requiring the development of legal agreements to reassure planning authorities that parking would not be displaced to neighboring districts. This in turn has necessitated the creation of legal bodies to administer and, in theory, enforce the "car-free declarations" that forbid personal car ownership.

9: CONCLUSIONS AND LESSONS LEARNED

The Netherlands' Vinex program for sustainable new growth lays out some principles that align with sustainable transportation policies, such as promotion of mixed-use development, accessibility of urban facilities by walking, bicycling or public transit, housing densities and conservation of green space. However, the program provides no regulations for pricing or limiting parking. As a result, Vinex locations such as Houten do not make an attempt to restrict parking.

Closing Thoughts

One last issue should be highlighted. These communities show that it is possible to create car-free and car-lite communities where people want to live. All of these developments are desirable places to live, and some are so desirable that they are experiencing an affordability crisis. In San Francisco, rents and housing prices have escalated dramatically throughout the Bay Area region, and San Francisco is now one of the most expensive cities in the world. The Market and Octavia area has especially high housing demand, making it one of the most expensive neighborhoods in one of the most expensive cities in the world. Thus, moving forward, a key reality of livability is that it becomes more exclusive under conventional market organization. The demand for San Francisco's Market and Octavia, and for urban living in cities from Amsterdam to Stockholm is almost insatiable. There will need to be public interventions such as those the GWL Terrain model has implemented to make these places not only livable, but equitable, for all.

We not only need to make more low car(bon) communities, but we need to make sure they are inclusive.

We are figuring out how the environmental sustainability component of cities works, but there is work to be done on the socioeconomic dimension of sustainability.

Index

affordable housing 49–50, 66–67, 152–153; social housing 7, 9, 14, 111, 127, 135
Amsterdam 7–9, 15, 18–22; *see also* GWL Terrein
analysis *see* quantitative analysis
automobility *see* car use

Beatley, T. 23
bicycles 144, 148; GMV 117, 122–123; GWL Terrein 10–12, 18, 20–21; Hammarby Sjöstad 79, 87–89; Houten 125–131, 133, 135–139; Market and Octavia 43, 57–60, 70; Västra Hamnen 95–96, 106; Vauban 30, 33–35
bike sharing 60, 72, 79, 81, 133, 148
Bo01 *see* Västra Hamnen
Broaddus, A. 23
Brook, D. 17
building design 8, 18, 50–51, 73, 100–102
buses 30, 57, 62, 68, 70, 85, 95, 97, 104, 115, 116, 133, 148
businesses 14, 27, 48, 51, 69, 85, 102, 132, 150

Calatrava, S. 91–93, 99, 102
California 45, 65; *see also* Market and Octavia
car ownership 1, 143–145; GMV 121; GWL Terrein 8–9, 16, 20; Hammarby Sjöstad 87; Houten 135, 140; Market and Octavia 61–62, 67; Västra Hamnen 105; Vauban 33–36
car use 1–2, 33, 121, 137–139, 146–147
carbon emissions *see* GHG emissions
car-free declaration 17
carsharing 16–17, 32, 35–36, 60, 81, 99, 117, 134, 149
case studies 2–4, 141–145
Central Freeway 40, 43, 44, 46, 49, 56, 57, 71
Cervero, R. 3, 23
China 1
CHP 18, 120
Christiaanse, K. 9
cities 2, 4–5, 149–150
combined heat and power *see* CHP
commercial sector *see* businesses
community 17–18, 23–25, 28, 37, 55–56, 69, 151–153
commuting 62–63, 88, 106–107, 123–124, 137–139
comparative analysis 141–145

congestion charge 75, 78, 86, 88, 90, 111, 122, 147, 151
Contreras, A. 45, 54
curbside parking 48–49, 82–83, 146

demand management 38, 151; *see also* transportation demand management
density 19–20, 61–62, 87, 105, 150
Derks, R. 126
design *see* policy and design; urban design
development *see* planning
disability program 85
distance traveled 2, 21, 63–64, 106–107, 138–139

Ecoplan 9, 17
educational programs 134
emissions *see* GHG emissions
employer contributions 134
energy 1–2, 18, 32, 85–86, 103, 120
environmental goals 9, 17–18, 72–73, 107, 110; *see also* resource use
Erskine, R. 92, 99, 117–118

ferry service 79
filtered permeability 126, 148
Flagghusen 94, 102–103
flexible carsharing 17
freeway 42–44, 46, 49–51, 56–57, 65–71
freeway revolt 43
Freiburg 23–25, 30–36; *see also* Vauban
fuel prices 5

General Plan 45
gentrification 7, 49–50, 66–67, 69, 152–153
Geuze, A. 9
GHG emissions 1–2, 21, 40, 65, 78, 86, 89, 99, 144–145
global warming 1, 5
GMV 109–111, 123–124, 141–143, 146–150, 152; planning 111–113; policy and design 114–120; quantitative analysis 120–123
government policies 152
greenhouse gases *see* GHG emissions
Greenwich Millennium Village *see* GMV
groceries 14, 21, 27, 51, 106, 107, 120, 122, 123, 137, 139, 140, 149

INDEX

Grüne Flotte 32
GWL Terrein 7–8, 22, 141–147, 150–151; planning 8–9; policy and design 9–18; quantitative analysis 18–21; resource use 18

habits 102–103
Hammarby Sjöstad 72–73, 89–90, 141–145, 149–150; planning 73–75; policy and design 75–86; quantitative analysis 86–89
Hayes Valley 41, 43, 44–45, 48, 50, 51, 54–55, 66, 67–68, 69, 70
home working 12, 111, 123, 124, 150; telecommuting 61, 62
housing 12–14, 27, 83–84, 102, 132; affordable 49–50, 66–67, 152–153; live/work units 111–112, 123–124, 150; Vinex 127, 129, 135, 152
Houten 125–126, 139–148, 150, 152; planning 126–127; policy and design 127–134; quantitative analysis 134–139

impact fees 45–46, 50, 55–56, 66, 69, 148, 152
interagency coordination 68–69, 75–76

jobs 21, 27, 37, 40, 48, 56, 64, 65, 87, 94, 140, 149, 150; see also commuting; live/work units

Koepelvereniging 17–18, 22
Kohlhoff & Kohlhoff 24

land use 12–14, 27–28, 51, 83–85, 120, 132, 150
livability 2, 7, 23, 26, 43, 50, 67, 69, 72, 153
live/work units 111–112, 123–124, 150
London 109, 111, 113–116, 120–123; see also GMV

Malmö see Västra Hamnen
Market and Octavia 40–43, 64–71, 141, 143–153; planning 44–46, 65; policy and design 46–60; quantitative analysis 60–64
masterplanning 23, 24, 26, 37, 45, 60, 73, 124, 149, 150, 151
methodology see case studies
Milton Keynes 134–138
mobility management 95, 102–103, 107; see also transportation demand management
mode share 143–144; GMV 121–123; GWL Terrein 20–21; Hammarby Sjöstad 87–89; Houten 137–138; Market and Octavia 62–63; Västra Hamnen 105–106; Vauban 33–35

national planning 72, 150–153
No Ridiculous Car Journeys 103

Octavia Boulevard 40, 42–43, 46, 49–50, 67, 68
off-street parking 47–48, 82–83, 146
on-street parking 48–49, 82–83, 146
one-way carsharing 16, 17, 81
Øresund Bridge 97–98
OV-chipkaart 15, 133
OV-Fiets 133
Oyster Card 116

parking 144–146, 151; GMV 114–115; GWL Terrein 15–16, 20; Hammarby Sjöstad 81–83; Houten 129, 135, 139–140; Market and Octavia 44–45, 47–49, 67; Västra Hamnen 97–99, 107; Vauban 23–26, 36–37
parklets 54–55
participatory planning 17–18, 36–37, 151; see also community
pedestrian infrastructure 29–30, 60, 79–80, 95–96, 117, 126–127, 147
planning 150–151; GMV 111–113; GWL Terrein 8–9; Hammarby Sjöstad 73–75, 89–90; Houten 126–127; Market and Octavia 44–46, 65, 68–69; Västra Hamnen 93–94; Vauban 23–25
policy and design 145–153; GMV 114–120; GWL Terrein 9–18; Hammarby Sjöstad 75–86; Houten 127–134; Market and Octavia 46–60; Västra Hamnen 94–104; Vauban 25–32
Proposition 13 55
public bikes 133
public space 10–12, 28, 51–55, 83, 100, 118–119, 132
public transport 148–149; GMV 115–116, 121–123; GWL Terrein 15; Hammarby Sjöstad 75–79, 87–89; Houten 133; Market and Octavia 56–57, 69–70; Västra Hamnen 97; Vauban 30–36, 38
quantitative analysis: GMV 120–123; GWL Terrein 18–21; Hammarby Sjöstad 86–89; Houten 134–139; Market and Octavia 60–64; Västra Hamnen 104–107; Vauban 33–37

INDEX

The Randstad 125, 140; *see also* Houten
RegioKarte 31, 36, 38
renewable energy 86, 104, 110
residential buildings *see* housing
residents' views 36–37, 151
resource use: GMV 120; GWL Terrein 18; Hammarby Sjöstad 85–86; Västra Hamnen 103–104; Vauban 32
Rieselfeld 23, 24, 33–35, 143, 151
Rotne, G. K. S. 98

San Francisco *see* Market and Octavia
San Francisco Municipal Transportation Agency *see* SFMTA
Section 106 111, 112–113, 114, 121, 152
SF-CHAMP 63–64
SFMTA 48, 56, 63, 68–69
Shoup, D. 4
site characteristics 141–143
Skånetrafiken 97
smartcards 15, 56, 77, 97, 116, 133, 149
StadtMobil 32
Stockholm 72–73, 75–79, 81–83, 85–90; *see also* Hammarby Sjöstad
street layout 10, 23, 26–27, 68, 83, 100, 118, 131
sustainable mobility report 95
sustainable resource use *see* resource use

Tham, K. 99–100
traffic 23, 43, 67–68, 125, 129, 146–148; *see also* congestion charge; street layout
trams 15, 30–31, 35, 75–77

transferability 4–5
transit *see* public transport
transport *see* bicycles; car use; public transport
transportation demand management 38, 151
travel distances 2, 21, 63–64, 106–107, 138–139
Turning Torso tower 91–94, 98, 102, 103, 105

umbrella organization 17–18
urban design 9–14, 26–28, 145–153; GMV 117–120; Hammarby Sjöstad 83–85; Houten 131–132; Market and Octavia 50–55, 68; Västra Hamnen 99–102
U.S. 1–2, 4–5, 40, 70–71; *see also* Market and Octavia

Västra Hamnen 91–93, 107–108, 141–145, 147, 149–150; planning 93–94; policy and design 94–104; quantitative analysis 104–107
Vauban 23, 37–38, 141–148, 150–152; planning 23–25; policy and design 25–32; resource use 32
vehicle miles traveled *see* VMT
Veldhuizen 135–138
Vinex locations 19–20, 127, 129, 135, 153
VMT 2, 4, 5, 61, 63–64, 145

waste 18, 85, 104
water 18, 86, 104, 120
World Bank 1

Zeist 134–135, 138